UNDERSTANDING THE FUTURE INTERNET

UNDERSTANDING THE FUTURE INTERNET

HERVÉ COUTURIER, BURKHARD NEIDECKER-LUTZ,
VASCO ALEXANDER SCHMIDT, AND DAN WOODS

Evolved
Technologist
Press
New York, NY

Understanding the Future Internet
Hervé Couturier, Burkhard Neidecker-Lutz, Vasco Alexander Schmidt, and Dan Woods

Copyright© 2011 by Evolved Media, LLC

Published by Evolved Technologist Press, an imprint of Evolved Media, 1375 Broadway Fl 3, New York, New York 10018

This book may be purchased for educational, business, or sales promotional use. For more information contact:

Evolved Technologist Press
(646) 827-2196
info@EvolvedTechnologist.com
www.EvolvedTechnologist.com

Editors: Dan Woods, Deb Cameron
Writers: Dan Woods, Kermit Pattison, Deb Cameron
Copyeditor: Deb Cameron
Production Editor: Deb Gabriel
Cover and Interior Design: 1106 Design
Illustrator: Deb Gabriel
First Edition: September 2011

ISBN: 0-9825506-4-2, 978-0-9825506-4-9

Contents

Acknowledgments

The International Research Forum would not have been possible without the help of many people. We benefitted from the assistance of many friends and colleagues and here take the opportunity to express our gratitude.

First, we would like to thank the participants of the **International Research Forum 2010.** These leaders from business, academia, and government started the discussion and generated many of the questions and observations discussed in this book. We are fortunate to have assembled such an impressive collection of people.

We also extend our gratitude to the people who made the forum a success. Many thanks to Sabine Patsch, Christiane Kubach, and to the rest of the SAP Research Communications team for their help organizing the event. Thanks also to moderator Dan Woods for asking provocative questions and keeping the discussion rolling along. Last but not least, we tip our hat to Lutz Heuser, former head of SAP Research, who deserves credit for being the animating force behind the IRF conference for many years.

This book represented a change of course from previous IRF books. Unlike past years, the lion's share of the work was done after the forum and we drew heavily upon the expertise of several key people within SAP. Two people in particular deserve special praise for their efforts. Burkard Neidecker-Lutz served as the brain trust behind this project and his acumen and insights are reflected on virtually every page. Vasco Alexander Schmidt served as the main project manager and worked diligently to chase down sources and information, thereby enriching the project with his thoughtful and deliberate care.

We also are grateful for the many experts who shared their wisdom in interviews after the forum. They included many colleagues within SAP Research and other parts of SAP. The interviewees who were not at the Forum itself are listed in the Appendix as virtual participants, and we thank them all.

The writing team of Dan Woods and Kermit Pattison turned the raw transcripts and interviews into a flowing narrative. Transcriptionists Richard Fisher and Tanya Boroff produced fast and accurate records of our conversations. Project manager Deb Gabriel coordinated interviews, kept track of multiple revisions, and kept all the parts of this project on track and on schedule. Managing editor Deb Cameron improved the manuscript in countless ways with her sharp editing eye. The text was enhanced with the illustrations by Deb Gabriel and the cover and interior design by Michele DeFilippo and her team at 1106 Design.

As always, we also are deeply indebted to the SAP Executive Board for their vision and support of this project.

Introduction

The Future Internet is going to affect us all. Today's Internet brought many changes to our personal lives. Social networking and the use of mobile applications are only two of several trends that inspire us and shape our lives. We all know that these trends will soon be adopted widely, making the Internet an even more far-reaching platform for doing business. But there are serious technical and political issues that must be dealt with on the way to the future of business on the Internet. This book is a primer on the Future Internet, providing a high-level summary of key issues. It is aimed at helping technology leaders, government officials, and the general public understand how the Future Internet will impact our lives and our work.

This book is a compendium of applied research that helps all those affected by the Future Internet to prepare for the future. It:

- Identifies trends related to the Future Internet and the related opportunities and threats

- Identifies solutions, technologies, and business models to deal with that trend. This includes both near-term solutions and next-generation solutions that "leapfrog" into the future

- Helps business executives and product managers anticipate trends and ask themselves key questions to help plan for the future

- Shows how Business Webs can serve as an organizing principle of the Future Internet. Business Webs are an incarnation of the Future Internet offering real-time trading networks that deliver end-to-end business services optimized for mobility and ease of participation

This book is an outgrowth of the **International Research Forum 2010,** an annual event sponsored by SAP Research. In May 2010, three-dozen participants gathered in Germany for the International Research Forum sponsored by SAP Research. They represented leading minds from the high-tech and telecommunications industries, from academia, and from governments. Participants came from Europe, Africa, Asia, the Americas, and Australia. For two days, these participants listened, learned, and debated. They sketched a broad vision for the Future Internet that, though necessarily hazy, gives us a preview of the road ahead.

Yet this book is not just an account of the proceedings (which are available online at: *http://www.international-research-forum.com/ WIKI_2010/index.php/Main_Page*). Instead, it provides highlights from those discussions and further explores the many interesting questions that were raised during the meeting of the minds that occurred during the **International Research Forum 2010** and describes SAP's position in the Future Internet ecosystem.

Hervé Couturier, Head of Business Information
Technology & Research at SAP AG

Primed for Disruption

This book serves as a primer on the Future Internet as envisioned by SAP. It seeks to educate both SAP employees and the public about the Future Internet and to provide a high-level summary of key issues.

This book has an ambitious but simply stated aim: to survey all of the issues that fall under the umbrella of the Future Internet so that practitioners, executives, government officials, analysts, and researchers have a better idea of what is coming and what will be important to their particular domains of interest.

- This chapter surveys the broad trends behind the Future Internet and explains why the Internet is evolving into a societal operating system. This chapter introduces the concept of business webs, a new paradigm for business computing that is likely to play a prominent role in the Future Internet

- Chapter 2 examines how the Future Internet will be designed and implemented

- Chapter 3 explores how the Future Internet will give rise to new business models and innovations

- Chapter 4 looks at where we are headed with the Future Internet

The first task is to acknowledge the inevitable changes in the road ahead. The Internet will no longer be an arena of specific capabilities such as ecommerce, email, enterprise applications, or company web pages; instead the Future Internet will be an omnipresent fact of life and virtually every aspect of the enterprise will be premised upon it. The business environment of the future will be distinguished by several characteristics. Business technology will:

- Rely on the Internet as a fundamental and critical infrastructure

- Bring consumers, governments, and business users together

- Manage data in real time

- Optimize access via mobile technology

- Behave like a social network for enterprises

This book helps us prepare for this disruption. The Future Internet is a matter of survival. Every company will face a stark choice: adapt to the Internet or go extinct. Businesses have faced mandates for change previously, such as with the arrival of the original Internet. This time the challenges are different. The Future Internet will bring new capabilities, new opportunities, and new threats. It will spawn novel applications and business models—and doom those companies that fall behind the times and fail to adapt.

Every enterprise must ask itself a key question: Will we be disrupted by a competitor or will we disrupt ourselves? This book prepares managers to confront these questions and gain the willingness and acumen to disrupt themselves—and to seize new opportunities before their competitors do.

Assembling the Puzzle: How to Think about Infrastructure, Platforms, Services, Applications, and Business Models

Let's step back and view the Future Internet in the context of technological evolution. Technology can be envisioned as a stack that consists of the following elements. (These definitions are not intended to be academically precise and are simple thumbnail descriptions to help us sketch out a conceptual framework.)

Infrastructure: The standardized, general-purpose foundation of the Internet that started with networking protocols and has grown to include capabilities for video on demand, email, location services, and so on.

Platforms: Collections of general-purpose components designed for certain types of systems. Platforms are less general and less standardized than infrastructure. They are usually built with the idea of creating one particular category of system.

Services: A specific, ready-to-use component that can be found and invoked by someone seeking to build or use a system. A service is more ready-to-use than an individual component. Services can be provided by technology or people.

Applications: A system built of services, platforms, and custom components for a task.

Business models: A way of organizing the delivery of a product or service that may be supported by applications.

These elements form a general technology stack as depicted in Figure 1-1. Solutions are built from the underlying layers of technology.

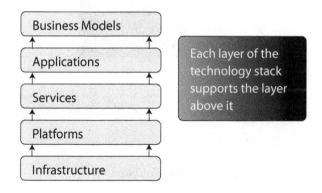

Figure 1-1. The General Technology Stack

This stack is constantly evolving. New-purpose components are developed at the higher layers and later become incorporated into the more general layers below. This occurs as applications lead to the discovery of reusable services or those that can be repurposed for multiple tasks, see Figure 1-2.

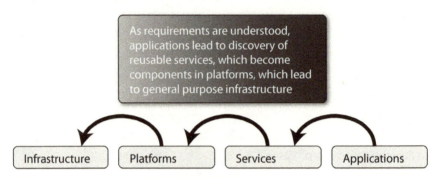

Figure 1-2. How Technology Evolves

This process occurs gradually (Figure 1-3). A technology may be developed as a component of a single application, turned into a reusable service, and eventually evolve into a platform and all-purpose infrastructure. In many cases, a specific component may span categories and thus not fit neatly into these conceptual categories.

Figure 1-3. The Fluid Reality

This model helps us understand the evolution of the Internet. The Internet began as a networking infrastructure with platforms and services built on top of it as indicated in Figure 1-4. These were used to build applications such as those that powered Web 1.0 and Web 2.0.

But, following the principles we just described, the cloud era began and the infrastructure absorbed much of the platform and services layer

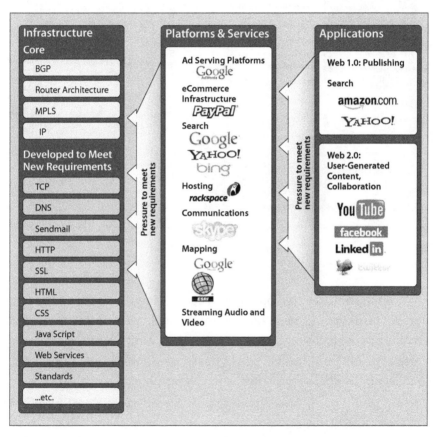

Figure 1-4. Challenges for the Future Internet Infrastructure

as indicated in Figure 1-5. More and more components were offered as a service: infrastructure as a service, platform as a service, applications as a service, and so on. As a result, applications were built on a broader, more sophisticated layer.

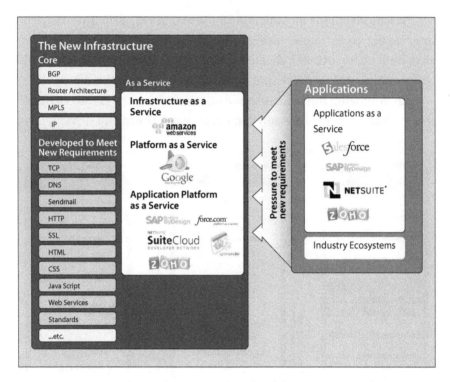

Figure 1-5. The Cloud Era

At first, this occurred opportunistically. Now, however, the ad hoc nature of this arrangement has become obsolete. The infrastructure is creaking as old technologies are nearing their limits. New technologies are appearing. Now the question is, how are we going to adapt that layer to meet all the challenges? How will we assemble these elements in an optimal combination? In this sense, the Future Internet represents a puzzle as shown in Figure 1-6.

Business webs, a paradigm created by SAP Research for how applications should be structured in the era of the Future Internet, present the next evolution of this process. Business webs represent a new paradigm for enterprise computing in which the Internet serves as a platform for a service-oriented approach and allows businesses to form networks. Business webs can be viewed as an assembly of all the pieces of the Future Internet into a coherent whole. Business webs will serve as the mesh that connects the infrastructure, platforms, services, and applications into

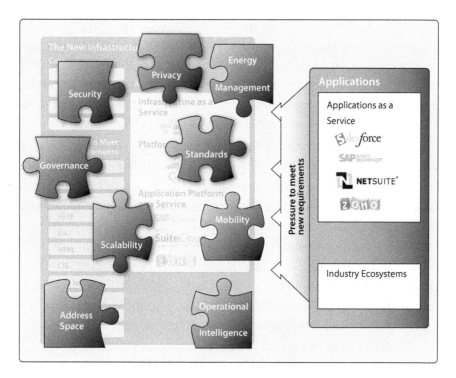

Figure 1-6. The Future Internet Puzzle

end-to-end business solutions. They will orchestrate these elements into packages that can easily be adopted by business users to suit the particular needs of a company. These building blocks will form the foundation of new business models as discussed in Chapter 3.

A new puzzle is coming into view—and this time the puzzle is much larger and the pieces are more complex. How will the puzzle of the Future Internet come together? What are the pieces? What are the problems in each area? How are the pieces related? This book explores these questions—and shows how the new arrangement of these puzzle pieces represents the essence of business webs.

What Is the Future Internet?

The Future Internet is a vision of a public infrastructure that goes beyond the Internet as we know it today. Over the next decade, the Internet will transform into a "seamless fabric" of classic networks and networked objects that connect to one another dynamically. These elements will be ubiquitous, always on, and unleash a deluge of real-time information. The Internet will become the new societal operating system that underlies every aspect of our lives, including business, government, and social interactions. The Future Internet will open a host of new opportunities and challenges, many of which will be explored in this book.

These changes are quickly making obsolete some key elements of the current Internet. Over the last 30 years, the Internet has both revolutionized human society and run far beyond its original scope. The current Internet was designed as a means to connect academic researchers and the military. From these humble beginnings, the Internet grew into something as integral to our lives as books, roads, telephones, and public utilities. It is becoming the primary medium for exchanging information, communication, and commerce. The Internet has become a critical infrastructure, like roads, railroads, mail, and phones in the last century. Simply put, it is the global network of the 21st century.

Yet the current Internet is hitting a ceiling. It is widely agreed that the current Internet will soon reach its limits in both architecture and capacity. Traffic has grown to the point where performance has begun to suffer and the number of participants causes the old Internet protocol to run out of address space. Short-term solutions no longer suffice. As one group of experts observed, "The truth is the Internet was never designed for how it is now being used and is creaking at the seams."[1]

The current Internet faces structural limitations such as scalability, flexibility, mobility, security, trustworthiness, and robustness of networks and services. At this point, connectivity still is not ubiquitous and bandwidth has limits. Devices cannot always talk to each other and content cannot be used across all devices. Applications and interfaces are still too complex and unintuitive. Users are vulnerable to spam, identity theft, and fraud. The Internet was designed as a network of academic and military participants who were assumed to be trusted parties; it did not anticipate the kinds of security threats and malevolent users we see

---

[1] "Future Internet 2020: Visions Of An Industry Expert Group," DG Information Society and Media Directorate for Converged Networks and Service, 2009, *http://www.future-internet.eu/fileadmin/documents/reports/FI_Panel_Report_ v3.1_Final.pdf*.

today. Dr. David Clark of MIT, one of the original architects of the Internet and an elder statesman, has warned that "the Internet is broken."[2] Dr. Clark points to several fundamental flaws: lack of security, weak traffic routing protocols, difficulty integrating new objects, and more. He has warned that disaster may be creeping upon us slowly—so slowly that the public fails to notice—and that performance may slip so much that the Internet's utility may stall or plunge downward.

All of this compels us to rethink fundamental aspects of the Internet so that it may continue to thrive into the 21st century. The Future Internet requires new architectures, new interfaces, new methods of data management, new means of integrating objects and networks, new devices, new business models, and new ways of behavior. It demands a ubiquitous network that expands capacity by orders of magnitude. It must be able to act as a full-service marketplace that can accommodate an ever-growing array of services. It must incorporate the ubiquitous devices, sensors, and voluminous data of the Internet of Things, distributed computing platforms, Web 2.0, peer-to-peer services, broadband access networks, and mobile devices, just to name a few. Somehow it must be regulated to ensure a trusted, fair, and secure place to do business. The Future Internet involves many stakeholders with many agendas. It is not simply a technical engineering problem; rather it is a matter with profound social, economic, political, and legal implications. All this compels us to rethink the basic Internet architecture conceived more than 30 years ago.

How Will the Future Internet Arrive?

The Future Internet is not some force that will arrive all at once like a tidal wave. Rather, it is a term that encompasses an array of changes on the horizon. It also represents a mandate for change.

Businesses lack the tools to fully leverage all the elements of the Future Internet. They need a new model for end-to-end integration of infrastructure and services. They need a means to orchestrate the disparate elements of the Future Internet into freely combinable applications and services that are accessible via the Internet and mobile technology.

---

[2] David Talbot, "The Internet is Broken," *MIT Technology Review*, Dec 2005/ January 2006, *http://www.technologyreview.com/printer_friendly_article .aspx?id=16356.*

The Future Internet will serve as a platform for a new web-based service economy. The Internet is moving beyond a business-to-consumer space and consumer-to-consumer space and becoming more of a business-to-business space. This business ecosystem is a key component of the vision of the Future Internet. We call such ecosystems "business webs."

This book approaches the Future Internet with an emphasis on business webs and the web-based service industry. It describes how the Future Internet will create value chains that link diverse participants in freely combinable deployment models, delivery channels, and business models. Complex business processes will become commodities that can be bought and sold via the Internet. This Future Internet will enable new global business networks that tie all facets of our personal and professional lives into one end-to-end system.

As limitations are overcome, we will witness the emergence of a new Internet, one that will serve as a platform for commerce. These business webs will knit together companies and business processes in entirely new ways. This will force us to think about a future in which everything we do must be adapted to business webs and the Future Internet. We will no longer speak of "Internet companies" as a separate class; *every* company will be obliged to become an Internet company. Every product and business process will be designed with the Internet in mind.

The Future Internet is a disruptive force that will dislodge established players, introduce new players, and change established practices. For example, we can no longer assume a world of multi-year end-user licenses and two- or three-year development cycles. Instead, we must brace for a world of subscription models where customers can depart at any time, and software development cycles are measured in months, not years. Many similar disruptions lurk ahead.

Every company will have to adapt its business model, even if it remains in the same industry. Companies must ask themselves how they can become solution providers for their customers. Some prominent companies have made this transition very successfully. For example, both IBM and HP transformed themselves from product companies into service providers. All companies must prepare themselves for the same kind of agile adaptation.

What is the Future Internet?

This book approaches the Future Internet from the perspective of business webs. But others have offered different perspectives on the Future Internet. Here is how some participants in the IRF 2010 summarized their view of the Future Internet:

"An enabling set of technologies, business models, and infrastructure to enable people, businesses, and the physical world to interact in the future."
—Rick Bullotta, Burning Sky Software

"A set of companies offering services, a set of companies governing data that is out there, and then a set of companies, probably very few of them, orchestrating services."
—Stephan Fischer, SAP

"A combined platform for social, business, and distributed computing, with a particular focus on networks and services."
—Stefan Tai, Karlsruhe Institute of Technology

"Continuing growth of the operating system for building applications in a network-connected, mobile world, but also the political, economic, and social governance mechanisms that need to be put in place in order to allow growth to occur."
—Dan Woods, CITO Research

"It's the classical Web 2.0 plus the Internet of Things and Internet of Services, leveraging completely new business models, so that a vendor could really leverage the data coming in from the Internet of Things and sell it through technologies or services of the Internet of Services."
—Uwe Kubach, SAP Research

"The Future Internet will have individuals, crowds, and applications driving it, rather than improved business models. Sure, people will be making money from it. But the drive will come from unexpected directions."
—Paul Hawking, Victoria University

"It's about interoperable applications and services. Let me object to those of you who talk about a user-driven Internet of individuals—completely wrong. The users will use what's available and attractive. The money and the value will be in making sure you have the right tools, which are the applications and services. What is the whole beauty of Apple? It's the tools."
—Lutz Heuser, AGT International

(continued on next page)

(continued from previous page)

"The Future Internet is going to be the way that everyone communicates. We won't have a separate telecommunications network. All communications, all connectivity between humans and things, will happen over the Internet. The Future Internet will be the mechanism that connects both people and things."

—David Skellern, National ICT Australia

Why Should We Care?

Why should we worry about the Future Internet? Granted, we have reason to be skeptical because we constantly hear prognosticators talking about the next big thing, the much-hyped megatrend that never quite pans out, and the hot new product that is mostly the figment of marketers' imaginations. This book does not attempt to predict the future—indeed anybody who does is bound to be wrong. But it does raise crucial questions that deserve attention. The Future Internet is an umbrella term that encompasses a wave of changes on the horizon. Anybody in any business ought to be concerned about these matters.

The main reason to pay attention to the issues discussed in this book can be summed up simply: the Future Internet is becoming our societal operating system.

The Internet is no longer just technical infrastructure. It is an information processing resource that is able to capture—and multiply—human intelligence and information from myriad sources. The term "societal operating system" reflects the breadth and power of the Future Internet. It combines conceptual elements such as the social operating system (social networking platforms and applications), Internet operating system (a concept championed by Tim O'Reilly and others), and business operating system (enterprise software and commerce). The Internet has grown to the point where it now permeates every aspect of our lives, including the economy, communications, and even social interaction. Virtually every important activity now has an online equivalent. In some industrial environments, the entire process has moved online, making the original "real-world" equivalent obsolete. As such, the Internet is no longer an operating system at just a technical level. Instead, it has become *the* operating system at all levels of human society and commerce—and therefore raises issues about public policy, governance, regulation, interoperability, access, and so on.

For businesses, the Future Internet is important because it will lead to new capabilities—new components and services that can be used to create new applications and business models. It accelerates the speed of change and that is why it also brings new risks and threats to businesses. The Future Internet is not just an academic issue: it is also a matter of business and survival.

These are not minor questions to be left to the IT department. Rather, the Future Internet represents major strategy issues for top-level executives. CEOs must think about the strategic direction and the future of the Internet. The same holds true for public policy: senior officials, even heads of state, must address these questions. Granted, CEOs and heads of state may not be able to directly impact some aspects of the Future Internet, such as the change from one Internet protocol to another. But they must understand the issues because they will be confronted with making strategic decisions about these trends.

The Future Internet is going create new capabilities that will enable your business—or your competitor's business—to do things it cannot do now. For example, the rise of Amazon caused massive disruption in the book industry that put one-time giants out of business. But this was just the beginning. Amazon wrought changes that extended far beyond just the selling of retail books, such as services, acting as a vendor for other publishers, printing on demand, electronic books via the Kindle, selling many kinds of goods, and cloud computing.

Pondering the Future Internet

The Future Internet may lead to new capabilities to create new applications and business models.

The new components and services of the Future Internet can accelerate your ability to adapt to changing market conditions.

An understanding of the Future Internet will provide a competitive advantage.

Public officials must pay close attention because the Future Internet will become a critical part of the public infrastructure. The fiber optic cables of the Future Internet will become interwoven with every fiber of modern society. More and more government services will be provided via the Internet. There is public pressure to regulate it just as other key industries such as banking, utilities, or transportation are regulated today.

Governments that make wise choices about the Future Internet will enhance their economies, improve competitive standing, and offer their citizens a better quality of life, education, services, and protections.

New Business Webs

Business webs represent a new paradigm for enterprise computing in the Future Internet. By organizing our thinking around the concept of business webs, we will be able to better understand the pragmatic impact of the design, policy, and implementation issues involved in the Future Internet. Business webs take a service-oriented approach, deliverable over the Internet, thus allowing enterprises to organize into networks. These webs will include services like business intelligence, business network orchestration, Internet applications and services, mobile computing and user experience, security and trust, software engineering and tools, and technology infrastructure. These tools will be available to both large businesses and small ones. Business webs will be completely scalable, from large multinationals to local family businesses. Because these services are delivered over the Internet—which today is as ubiquitous as the telephone—there will be very low barriers to entry. These services would allow companies to engage in business as easily as Facebook allows people to connect with friends. There will be a menu of possibilities and every business will compose its own solution from these choices. The building blocks must have the capability to evolve continuously without the disruptive upgrades and reinstallations of yesteryear's software.

These webs will allow end-users to connect to each other, services, and applications more easily. The software will be deliverable over the Internet and extend the reach and power of enterprise systems. In short, these business webs fully exploit the power of the Internet by facilitating connections and exchange of information.

Business webs will serve as a cloud infrastructure for business applications optimized for mobile users. They will combine services from infrastructure providers, telecommunication carriers, and application providers into a seamless package available via the Internet and mobile networks. These real-time networks will supply all the necessary infrastructure, technology, applications, and information to provide complete end-to-end solutions for business users.

We already see many examples of emerging new breeds of Internet companies that fit this model: the rapidly-growing "app" and API economy, the web-based service economy, cloud computing, and a myriad of "as a service" offerings.

These new companies are crucibles of innovation. As we shall see in the discussion of business models in Chapter 3, most breakthroughs come not from product innovations but from process innovations. In other words, somebody figures out how to combine various elements to deliver a service or product more efficiently, economically, and easily. Business webs provide a platform to allow customers to do just that.

Business webs represent the next phase in the evolution of the Internet. First came the Internet of the 1990s, which was characterized by distribution of content to end-users. Next came business applications such as

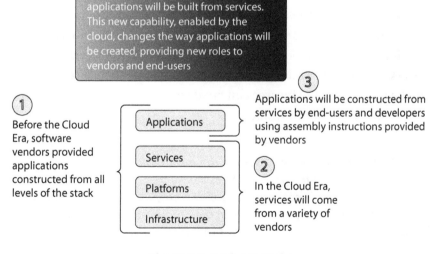

Business webs refer to the new way that applications will be built from services. This new capability, enabled by the cloud, changes the way applications will be created, providing new roles to vendors and end-users

① Before the Cloud Era, software vendors provided applications constructed from all levels of the stack

Applications
Services
Platforms
Infrastructure

③ Applications will be constructed from services by end-users and developers using assembly instructions provided by vendors

② In the Cloud Era, services will come from a variety of vendors

Figure 1-7. Business Webs

the digitization of sales in the form of ecommerce. The new millennium brought social networks like Twitter and Facebook. The business webs of the Future Internet are the next iteration and will merge these forces by combining B2B networks with social networks.

Several forces drive business, including the cloud, the Internet of Services, the proliferation of mobile devices, and the Internet of Things.

Business on the Future Internet: The Driving Forces

The expansion of social networks to business groups: Industry-specific social networks will enable broader cross-company collaboration between people and processes. They will encompass the full spectrum of dimensions including individual skills, hierarchical structures, and client relations.

Shorter development cycles: The development cycle for business applications will shorten dramatically. It will no longer be practical to think of two-year development cycles. In the future, it will be more appropriate to think of two-month development cycles. We can already see these new forces at work in the App Store. We should view business webs as platforms that facilitate the development of new business applications.

Real world, real time: The Internet will increasingly reflect the real world. The Internet of Things and the Internet of Services will continue to push the digital domain into the physical world of goods and services. Companies will have closer connections to their environment and more real-time information.

Taken together, these trends open vast opportunities for new business models. The pieces of the Future Internet are coming into place. The remaining question is: How will the pieces of this puzzle be arranged? This is the key business challenge of the Future Internet. If these challenges can be met, global businesses can create a fertile new ecosystem—the future "Business Mobile Cloud."

The Future Internet will change the most basic aspects of our daily lives, even a trip to the grocery store.

Like many young mothers, Maria lives a busy life. After dropping off her children at school, she hurries to the grocery store. On her way into the store, she grabs a shopping cart that is equipped with an electronic reader. Maria is a regular customer. Her car keys identify her to the shopping cart, which automatically downloads her shopping list.

The cart screen helps Maria navigate the aisles and acts like an in-store GPS system that guides her to each item on her list in an efficient sequence. Maria picks up two packages of spinach and wonders which one is fresher. She uses the SemProm (semantic product memory) browser to scan the items and pull up their digital product memories, which show the farms where they were grown, the dates when they were harvested, and the conditions under which they were stored and transported. She discovers that one package was grown at a local farm and is two days fresher. Before making up her mind she checks the organic certification. Satisfied, she puts the item in her cart.

In the next aisle she shops for a loaf of fresh bread. But her husband is allergic to gluten and she must carefully check the ingredients. She finds one loaf labeled gluten free and uses the browser to check the ingredients and the provenance of the flour.

Maria continues through the store and collects all the items on her list. When she is ready to check out, she once again pulls out her car keys, which carry her credit card information. She scans it on a reader device, verifies the amount of the electronic deduction, and carries the grocery bags to her car.

Oops. As Maria drives from the parking lot, she realizes she had forgotten to add an item on her list—the fresh strawberries that her children requested when she dropped them at school. Once again, the Future Internet comes to the rescue. The car's navigation system checks Maria's route home and finds a store on the way that carries the item. But the system also reminds her not to dally too much on extra errands. It's a hot summer day and the system senses the temperature and warns Maria she need to get home in a certain amount of time or else her ice cream will melt.

A New Frontier

Business webs open new frontiers for business. One of these frontiers is orchestration of the services of the business webs. One of the main achievements of ERP systems has been the creation of standardized processes for different elements of business. The Future Internet demands a new form of standardization and coordination. This time, however, the delivery model will no longer be installed application software. Instead, it will be services.

The questions are: How are those services going to evolve? Who will orchestrate and assemble these capabilities? Who will render the pieces into building blocks and allow customers to compose their own solutions?

Business webs address a gap in the market. Today, we can envision the Internet as a cloud where four elements meet: private businesses, public users, infrastructure, and mobile apps. Business webs can serve as a platform that leverages all of these elements—giving birth to applications like real-time trading systems or a mobile business cloud. At this point, however, this vision still lacks many key ingredients—and these shortcomings must be filled in order to bring this vision to reality. There is a keen need for an orchestrator to help businesses manage the complexity of the Future Internet.

This opens a huge opportunity. An orchestrator can provide application and technical services, business services (for example, the Internet of Services) as well as infrastructure, and offer end-to-end orchestration. It can process information like context data (weather or traffic, for example), enterprise data (traditional ERP information), and data from the Internet of Things. The platform can knit these elements together into a usable suite of services and optimize it for mobile users, an ever-growing segment of future users. As a result, new roles, customer niches, and business opportunities will emerge.

In the 1970s and 1980s, ERP solved the problem of uniting diverse technologies into coherent packages that allowed businesses to communicate around the world. A similar approach is needed now. Although today's technologies are more advanced, a similar federated approach is required that unites these new capabilities into components that can be combined, mixed, and matched as needed. This is the essence of business webs: creating new systems that incorporate legacy, current, and yet-to-be invented technologies into combinable building blocks that can be adapted to the next generation of enterprise environments.

The key message boils down to this: be prepared to deal with these forces or be displaced by your competitors. Waves of change are coming—your boat may be swamped if you are not ready.

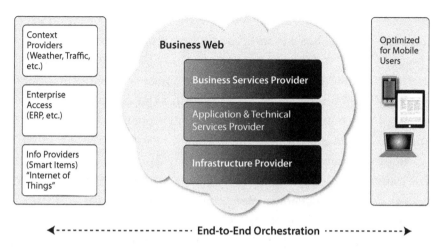

Figure 1-8. A Business Web as an Intermediary

Signs of Strain: A Look at Internet Infrastructure

All is not well at the lowest level of basic infrastructure. The infrastructure has been neglected for many years and, as a result, there will be widespread pain in the years ahead. Internet architecture is steadily losing its simplicity and transparency. It is widely agreed that the current Internet will soon reach both its architectural and capacity limits.

Growth. The Internet now has 2 billion users and the US National Science Foundation predicts this number will grow to 5 billion by 2020, with the greatest increase in developing nations. According to estimates by Minnesota Internet Traffic Studies (MINTs), Internet traffic increases by 50% each year. This amounts to a 100-fold increase every decade. Although the growth rate has slowed in recent years, it still represents a staggering increase in year-over-year traffic.

Bandwidth. The cost of providing bandwidth is falling. But the revenue from providing bandwidth is falling even faster. As a result, providers have little incentive to provide new bandwidth infrastructure to accommodate growing traffic.

Address space. The current Internet largely rests on Internet Protocol version 4 (IPv4), which allows for 4.3 billion unique addresses. When IPv4 was specified, it was deemed more than adequate but today more people and devices are coming online by the minute; as of February 2011 the address space has run out. The successor to IPv4 is IPv6. IPv6 has enough address space for every atom on the surface of earth—plus 100 more earths. But there is no consensus on a plan or timeline for migration to this new protocol. The likely scenario is that companies will have to install ugly band-aid solutions. They will probably have to run IPv4 and IPv6 at the same time.

Routing reliability. Routing remains the Achilles heel of the Internet. The Internet is actually a combination of many interconnected networks managed by different entities. Routers are required at every level to direct packets in the right direction. They rely on "routing tables" to know where to send certain types of information, such as sending emails via internal intranet versus the external Internet. But these routing tables are easily hijacked.

This allows governments to censor or block Internet traffic to quell dissent or free expression. For example, during the political unrest in Egypt in early 2011, the Egyptian government turned off the Internet for several hours. In April 2010, about 15% of the world's Internet prefixes were hijacked by a set of servers owned by China Telecom. Popular websites such as *dell.com, cnn.com,* and *amazon.de* were briefly re-routed through Chinese networks before reaching their destinations. In February 2008, Pakistan Telecom hijacked all YouTube traffic and took YouTube offline for two hours.

The rapid growth and fragmentation of core routing tables remains a pressing challenge for the Future Internet, especially if businesses rely on this infrastructure—a problem that will only grow as the number of hosts and networks continues to expand.

Domain Name System. The Domain Name System (DNS) is fragile and lacks security. One potential solution is implementing the DNS Security Extensions (DNSSEC) standard. But this will be an expensive process and must be done globally.

DNS queries are usually routed with User Datagram Protocol (UDP), but this only provides responses under 512 bytes. Domain names with DNSSEC enabled exceed this limit, obliging networks to ask for another DNS response using Transmission Control Protocol (TCP). DNSSEC can accommodate larger blocks of information, but response times are two to four times longer than the average non-DNSSEC query. One 2008 study by the ICANN Security and Stability Committee found that just 25% of routers tested were fully DNSSEC compatible, meaning they were able to both route and proxy DNS traffic using TCP or UDP with messages over 4096 bytes.

Even if corporations were to upgrade routers, the problem is likely to persist in the general public because home users are less likely to invest in expensive routers.

These signs of strain are not going away, given continued growth in Internet usage. A complete coverage of all these issues is beyond the scope of this book, but with a basic awareness of some of the technical problems you will be able to begin a discussion about how to prepare your organization for the future. Key topics will be discussed in greater depth in Chapter 2.

Opportunities for the Future Internet

The infrastructure problems described are real and must be solved at a technological level. Change is hard but well worth it considering the panoply of opportunities ahead, including the Internet of Things, the Internet of Services, the changes brought by mobility, and the trend toward cloud computing.

Internet of Things

In the future, the Internet will not be just a network of computers but also will incorporate billions of devices including mobile phones, embedded units in industrial equipment, RFID tags, and everyday objects such as cars and washing machines. The Internet of Things (IOT) rests on the premise that virtually every physical thing in the world can be connected to the Internet. In this vision, almost every physical object can be described digitally and read by machines.

The IOT goes by many names, such as pervasive computing or ubiquitous computing. All capture the same basic idea—a globally interconnected network with millions or billions of small nodes permeating every aspect of the physical world. The IOT goes far beyond the embedded systems proliferating in our world today. Embedded systems are becoming more commonplace in factories and devices; 90% of processors now go into devices other than traditional laptop or desktop computers.

The IOT represents a significant force in the business world. Forrester Research predicts that the total market for IOT technologies will sustain a growth rate of 48% and exceed US $11.5 billion by 2012.

Internet of Services

The Internet is becoming the platform for the global service economy. The Internet of Services is extending traditional service-oriented architecture. It is allowing businesses to reach new markets, gain new efficiencies, form partnerships, tap long-tail business models, and more. The infrastructure barriers to doing business in the Internet of Services are dropping rapidly. Software as a service, cloud computing, and other trends are democratizing innovation as never before. We are moving into a new frontier in the Internet of Services at the same time that industries are outgrowing traditional frameworks and need better ways to leverage the Future Internet.

Mobility

Mobile technology is exploding. The number and variety of mobile devices continues to multiply. Workers have gone beyond email and text and are now using smart phones and other mobile devices for more complex applications such as business intelligence and analytics. This trend will only increase and future applications must be optimized for mobile devices such as smartphones, laptops, iPads, and the next generation of portable communications.

The market for mobile business applications will continue to boom. It is expected to grow on many fronts: business-to-business and business-to-consumer services, e-government services for citizens, and mobile-to-mobile services like smart metering.

The Future Internet will increasingly be a mobile network. According to IDC, more than 1.2 billion workers worldwide—more than one-third of the workforce—will be using mobile technology by 2013.[3]

---

[3] "Worldwide Mobile Worker Population 2009–2013 Forecast," IDC, 2009.

Cloud Computing

Cloud computing is a disruptive force that is changing the nature of business computing. More and more companies are purchasing infrastructure and software as a service via the Internet. This has lowered barriers to entry and allowed new players to quickly enter markets and scale up. It also has facilitated business webs and partnerships. The cloud model will transform business services and enterprise computing. The cloud model will continue to expand into new arenas and commoditize other services.

The Future Internet Research Agenda

Much work remains to be done to bring the Future Internet vision to reality. Outside the business world, which tends to take a short- to medium-term perspective, a number of government and academic research initiatives are looking at more long-term, paradigm-shifting questions. Large investments are being made in Europe, North America, and Asia. The research agendas underscore the urgency of fixing the current shortcomings and developing this infrastructure. This section outlines the research agenda and describes some of the leading research initiatives.

Europe

Europe has taken the lead in identifying the Future Internet as a public priority. In fact, the term Future Internet is used widely in Europe and much less frequently in the US. On the continent, Europeans speak in terms of a European "digital agenda," a vision of a single online marketplace that unites the whole continent.[4] The digital agenda is one of the pillars of the EU 2020 vision of a new economy espoused by EU President José Manuel Barroso. The Future Internet is a key component of this vision.

European technology leaders tend to see the Future Internet as a vector for boosting the competitiveness of its information and communications technology sector and its economy in general. They hope

---

[4] "Europe's Digital Agenda," European Commission Information Society, *http://ec.europa.eu/information_society/digital-agenda/index_en.htm.*

that Europe can take the lead in developing the Future Internet and have pooled resources and pursued initiatives and tools toward that goal.

In Europe, we see a wide array of funding schemes: long- and short-term, academic, industrial, exploratory, experimental, fundamental, applied, innovation-oriented, product-oriented, and so on. There are Future Internet initiatives and policies on many levels: EU-wide, national, regional, state, and local. Major Future Internet initiatives are underway in countries such as Germany, France, Spain, Finland, Sweden, Belgium, Luxembourg, the Netherlands, Ireland, and Italy. These efforts look at the full spectrum of the Future Internet, from basic infrastructure to applications to business platforms.

Early one weekday morning, Henri wakes up in his smart home.

His smartphone briefs him on his agenda for the day: an early meeting at work, a report due at noon, and preparation for an out-of-town business trip at the end of the week. It also reminds him to leave early for his evening soccer match.

He shuffles into the kitchen and finds a hot cup of coffee waiting for him in the espresso maker. He sips and scans his news feeds on a laptop on the kitchen counter.

When he leaves, the security system on his condominium arms itself. The smart meter turns down the heating system and water heater to save energy while Henri is at work. They will warm up again just before it is time for him to return home in the evening.

His appliances can talk to each other. As he prepares to commute to work, his car navigation system comes to life and checks local traffic conditions. Today there is construction on his normal route to work, so the system suggests he take an alternative route.

During the evening, his electric car has been charging in the driveway. Henri has signed up for a plan with his local utility to buy wind-generated power generated by offshore turbines, which tend to produce the most power in the late evening or early morning. His smart meter allows him to recharge the car when power is cheapest.

The European Commission funds more than 100 projects spanning the full range of Internet architecture. These efforts focus not only on components and hardware, but also the application layers and social and economic aspects of the Future Internet.

European Commission Funded
Future Internet Projects and Initiatives

The Future Internet Public-Private Partnership (PPP): An initiative between the public sector and major Internet, communications, and technology companies. This is a prime example of the European federated approach. The EC has funded this initiative with 300 million euros for 2011–2013, supplemented by an R&D budget of 200 million euros. The PPP will explore specific scenarios like smart energy, healthcare, logistics, and smart living. *(http://ec.europa.eu/information_society/activities/foi/events/fippp/index_en.htm)*

THESEUS / TEXO (THESEUS) (Future Information Internet, Germany): Researches ways to navigate enormous volumes of Internet data. Oriented mainly to laying the groundwork for the Internet of Services. TEXO is a THESEUS project oriented toward providing a platform to make services tradable on the Internet. *(http://www.theseus-programm.de/default.aspx)*

ICT – Shok Research Programme (Finland): Developing future Internet networking technologies and seeks to create new global ICT-based business ecosystems. *(http://www.futureinternet.fi/)*

National Future Internet Initiatives GRIF (NFII-GRIF) (Research Group for the Future Internet, France): A collaboration between government, business, and universities to explore Future Internet opportunities and create three "laboratories of excellence" in Paris, Brittany, and Sophia.

IdF (Spain): Initiative involving public and private Internet-related organizations in application areas (for example, health) and technology platforms.

Ambient (Sweden): Future Internet initiative with six research tracks. *(http://www.cefims.eu/2011/01/sweden/)*

European Future Internet Alliance (EFIA): Industry-led group that facilitates focused research, development, and innovation toward the Future Internet. *(http://initiative.future-internet.eu/)*

FIRE (Future Internet Research & Experimentation): European Commission-funded research program that conducts long-term research and large scale testing for futuristic architectures, including "clean slate" and disruptive paradigms.

North America

In the US, we see a different sensibility. It has no broad umbrella initiative like the PPP. The government funds several important basic research efforts, but on applied research, the US has taken a more laissez-faire approach and left the private sector to its own devices.[5] The most prominent research efforts tend to be academic initiatives that focus on networking infrastructure and architecture. The notion of a "clean slate" approach (the idea of redesigning the Internet from scratch) animates much of the American basic research. In contrast, Europe has generally backed away from the clean slate idea and mostly turned toward an evolutionary approach and practical applications.

Some of the most important US research efforts focus on fundamental architecture.

US Funded Future Internet Initiatives

NeTS (Networking Technology and Systems): National Science Foundation (NSF) program focusing on networking research with a long-term orientation. It focuses on development of the science and technology advances needed to create next generation networks. The program included four parts: 1) FIND; 2) NBD (networking broadly defined); 3) ProWIN (programmable wireless networks); and 4) NOSS (networking of sensor systems). The program has been phased into NetSE, an NSF program oriented toward network research with a long-term focus and "clean slate" approach. *(http://www.cra.org/ccc/netse.php)*

FIND (Future Internet Design): A long-term initiative of the NSF NeTS research program that examines the requirements for a global network 15 years in the future. FIND explores how to design networks from scratch. It aims at comprehensive research of network architecture design. It supports many small projects and seeks to converge them into full-scale architectures. Those architectures will be tested on the GENI infrastructure. *(http://www.nets-find.net/)*

The Clean Slate program at Stanford University is a research effort to "reinvent the Internet." It aims to help the Future Internet overcome architectural challenges like scalability and mobility, integrate new technologies, and enable new applications and services. *(http://cleanslate.stanford.edu)*

---

[5] Lutz Heuser and Dan Woods, "Is Europe Leading the Way to the Future Internet." *IEEE Computing,* October, 2010, *http://citoresearch.com/content/europe-leading-way-future-internet.*

> **GENI:** A virtual laboratory for exploring future internets at scale. It seeks fundamental reconsideration of the service architecture. GENI is similar to the European FIRE (Future Internet Research & Experimentation) program, one of the few areas where there is an apples-to-apples comparison between European and US Future Internet programs. *(http://www.geni.net)*

Canada, not surprisingly, follows Europe more closely in its willingness to invest in research related to the Future Internet and seeks to join forces with European research initiatives. Evidence of this is the Canada-EU Future Internet Workshop, an annual event drawing researchers from Europe and many private sector and public sector Canadian groups.

Canada has been investing in Future Internet research for a long time under the auspices of CANARIE, a nonprofit corporation supported by the Canadian government *(http://www.canarie.ca/)*. Canada has funded leading-edge optical networking for many years; CANARIE's latest network, funded in 2002, is CA*Net4. At the same time, Canadian networking initiatives have been investing in optical Ethernet, laying fiber across the provinces. Evidence of the progress Canada has made in building a high-speed optical infrastructure is the fact that between October 2010 to January 2011, Canadian ISPs delivered Netflix traffic faster than all major US providers. (US providers delivered between 1400 and 2750 Kbps while Canadian ISPs, though fewer, delivered speeds between 2,800 to 3,200 Kbps consistently.)

Asia

Several important and well-funded Future Internet initiatives are underway in Asia.

> ### Asian Future Internet Initiatives
>
> **AKARI:** The AKARI project, run by the National Institute of Information and Communications Technology in Japan, explores designs for a new generation network. Like the US "Clean Slate" program, Akari also seeks to design a next generation network from scratch that will satisfy the demands of a ubiquitous networking society by 2020. It specifically avoids the notion of an incremental extension of the existing Internet and pursues a new-generation network architecture. *(http://akari-project.nict.go.jp/)*
>
> *(continued on next page)*

(continued from previous page)

JGN-X: An R&D test network operated by The Japanese National Institute of Information and Communications Technology for R&D collaboration of industry, academia, and government. *(http://www.jgn.nict.go.jp/)*

ASIA Future Internet Forum (Asia FI): Coordinates research and development on the Future Internet among countries in Asia. Conducts long term, open research by international collaboration. Working groups explore questions such as architecture, mobile, wireless, and testbeds. *(http://www.asiafi.net/)*

Future Internet Forum Korea (FIF Korea): Broad consortium of research efforts involving hundreds of experts on many fronts. *(http://fif.kr/)*

Designing and Implementing
the Future Internet

2

The Future Internet will become a critical infrastructure that underlies our work and professional lives. As such, it has strict requirements and design challenges. This chapter surveys these requirements—and notes those that remain major barriers. By better understanding the way that the Future Internet may emerge, the implications for each business and organization can be clearly understood.

The Future Internet may be viewed as a puzzle with many pieces. These pieces represent key elements such as privacy, security, Internet of Things, Internet of Services, and so on. The question is, how will these pieces be assembled? In this chapter, we look at individual puzzle pieces and the challenges for assembling them into a whole. As we analyze aspects of the Future Internet, we will identify capabilities that may appear in the short term and suggest the role that these capabilities may play in business webs. In many cases, there will be more questions than answers. Where possible, we describe potential solutions that appear feasible.

Requirements, Design Principles, and Barriers

To fulfill its vision, the Future Internet must fulfill the basic requirements of all the new uses that people will demand. Generally speaking, this means that it must extend beyond its current focus on data transport and connectivity and integrate additional functionalities in accord with its all-encompassing role as the societal operating system. Moreover, it must integrate these functionalities in a holistic manner—and not rely on band-aid solutions that are "patched in" as they have been in the past. Designers of products should consider these requirements in new product offerings.

In this chapter, we survey four major categories of challenges:

- General Requirements

- Architectural/Technical Requirements

- Business Requirements

- Software Development Requirements

General Requirements

General requirements for the Future Internet include security and trust, regulation and governance, and protection from cyberwar attacks.

Security and Trust

Virtually every list of requirements for the Future Internet puts security and trust at the very top of the wish list. Security may become one of *the* critical factors in the Future Internet.

Security remains an Achilles heel in the current Internet infrastructure. The original Internet was conceived at a time when the founders assumed that all computing systems were operated by trusted entities in a cooperative community of limited size. Today we find ourselves in a very different environment with viruses, spyware, phishers, hackers, spammers, malicious competitors, ID frauds and thieves, and other threats. The Internet has expanded to include the full range of humanity, good and bad. According to a report published by the European Commission Information Society, only 12% of European web users feel completely safe making online transactions.[6]

To truly fulfill its destiny as a societal operating system, the Future Internet must provide an environment that individuals and enterprises can trust. Enterprises will be loath to entrust the cloud with mission critical data without adequate protections. (In fact, some systems with fairly robust protections already exist but they are not widely used, such as pseudonymity, privacy preserving computation, and least authority systems.) The exchange of data should be as safe and easy as credit card transactions are today. The Future Internet must incorporate trust at all levels in all areas.

The Future Internet is becoming the platform for an ever-growing share of business, social, and personal transactions. People will use it to exchange the most sensitive data, including information about their private lives, finances, health, social lives, and so on. The strength of the Future Internet lies in information sharing and spontaneous interactions, even with entities that are previously unknown. This poses inherent risks of information being abused and data owners losing control over their data. How can this risk be mitigated? How can we make the Future Internet trustworthy and ensure that entities behave fairly and treat data according to the owners' preferences?

The first step is to be realistic about what we can and cannot do. We have to accept that there is no such thing as a completely secure Future Internet. This is a nirvana that is simply not attainable. Still, we can establish safety zones around the areas of greatest sensitivity, value, and vulnerability. Inevitably, some applications, domains, and resources will have higher risk exposure and others will have lower risk exposure. Low-risk areas can be established by integrating dedicated security services and restricting interaction to entities that are able to demonstrate their trustworthiness and allow governance or control by service consumers.

It is important to facilitate explicit risk considerations and protection needs for service and infrastructure consumers and providers. For

---

[6] "Digital Agenda For Europe," European Commission Information Society, *http://ec.europa.eu/information_society/digital-agenda/index_en.htm.*

instance, a person entering a social network may discover that its business model is based on personalized advertising that exploits location profiles. If this is explicitly disclosed, she can make an informed decision about whether to subscribe to the network or disclose personal information. Moreover, these policies must be made apparent in language that the average reader can quickly understand; the average person cannot comprehend 50 pages of legal and technical jargon.

Security and privacy do not come for free. We will have to pay a price in additional technology investments or restricted opportunities. The challenge is not to achieve a uniform security level for everyone and everything, but to provide the means to make the risks apparent and balance the needs.

Collaboration and Control

The Future Internet must facilitate information sharing in a dynamic fashion—on the fly, ad hoc, and across domains, applications, and heterogeneous devices and entities. In order to meet the demand for trusted collaboration and reduced risk, users need to determine with whom they will collaborate, and then express their mutual protection needs, impose controls, and enforce them.

Recent developments in privacy-preserving identity management schemes can provide useful tools. These schemes allow the disclosure of identity information to be "scaled" according to the requirements of the situation. Claims-based identification provides proof of only those identity properties and attributes that are necessary for the collaboration (for example, verifying that a user is above a minimum age). The technology for privacy-preserving identity management largely exists (for instance, OpenID or Microsoft's CardSpace), but has not been widely deployed. The heterogeneity of these technologies and devices poses another major challenge. A large-scale uptake of these technologies is needed to help the Future Internet realize its potential.

Similarly, a property-based approach can help establish trust in services. In this case, a service or company can be identified by not just its name, but also by properties that express its capabilities. Rich service descriptions might include security and privacy related attributes (verified by trusted parties) and provide information for a "service identity."

In fact, these service identities can be more meaningful than the actual name of the company. Such descriptions can serve as a container for expressing the service's protection levels and governance. If the user can express her policies in a similar, machine-processable way, these systems can match policies and decide if the service can be safely used.

Given the complexity and growth of the Future Internet, we must ensure that the above approach scales to multiple layers of dynamic collaboration. This motivates a data-centric security approach, in which policies are bound to data and travel with them. These are known as "sticky policies." Sticky policies allow for the expression of obligations, such as deletion or retention period, to be met by processing entities. For example, one recent proposal would allow people to preprogram an expiration date for photos posted on the web—an approach that might help people avoid the embarrassment of having their adolescent social network photos lingering on the Web for years and haunting them into adulthood. While the concept of "sticky policies" is theoretically pleasing, it faces practical challenges of performance and enforcement and requires further research and development.

Individuals leave a lifelong trail of data on the Internet but have little power to control how that information is used. For example, the PrimeLife research initiative seeks to create sustainable privacy and identity management to future networks and services. Funded by the European Commission's 7th Framework Programme, the project is investigating technologies to protect privacy and trust and life-long personal data trails without compromising on functionality.

The success of the measures above depends on enforcement mechanisms. Since traditional security mechanisms assume ownership of the controlled entity, the concept of enforcement has to be reconsidered for the Future Internet. It will be less about guaranteed security properties and more about providing incentives and deterrents to guide behavior. While there are technology and application scenarios that support enforcement (research in privacy-preserving computing has led to secure schemes for advanced scenarios like supply chain management, and trusted hardware is widely available but only rarely used), we believe that more lightweight schemes (such as monitoring and notification services) would serve the majority of protection needs. Research in this field, including both technical and non-technical controls (like codes of business conduct or regulatory frameworks), is strongly encouraged.

Extended Attack Surfaces and Emerging Threats

Like any other technology, the Future Internet rests on hardware and software infrastructure—and it has its own security flaws and vulnerabilities like any other infrastructure.

These threats may be amplified by the number of software components and means of interaction. These extend the attack surface and provide new means for attackers to penetrate a system. For example, attackers might launch malicious services interfaces that pretend to be legitimate services in order to attack their victims and gain entry into a system. The Future Internet is all about collaboration, data sharing, open architectures, and systems—all of which potentially means an increased level of vulnerability.

The general principles and best practices of avoiding vulnerabilities and countering threats still apply, but we need to bolster them with new approaches. We need a stricter discipline in enforcing them and supporting the service and application developer in building secure software and validating the security of their code. Given that distributed, on-demand platforms enable everybody to orchestrate services and build customized applications, we cannot expect full security awareness and an advanced level of security expertise. Hence, the platform should provide the required security services, make them easily consumable for developers, visualize the security requirements and constraints, and support threat analysis and risk assessment. Security engineering reaches across multiple abstraction levels, from orchestration (for example, by visualizing and validating security properties of business processes) to coding (for example, by providing input sanitization services following rigorous format specifications and supporting automated code analysis).

We cannot predict what new threats might emerge in the future. Attackers are creative, technically savvy, and command powerful, distributed resources. We already have seen new attacks for web applications like cross-site request forgery, HTTP verb tampering, and HTTP parameter pollution—and we should heed these warnings. There is no reason to believe that new Future Internet technologies will not attract attackers and lead to new assaults.

The community must monitor and analyze the evolving threat situation, asking for a more open and yet secure exchange of threat and attack data beyond the current vulnerability registers. Only with such a shared knowledge base will predictive threat analysis be successful and global attention be guided to the most critical resources, components, and technologies.

Toward an Economic Foundation of Security

Despite all the potential of the Future Internet, we cannot expect it to be entirely safe.

As Butler Lampson stated, "Security is not about perfection."[7] Instead, we must be realistic, discriminating, aware of risks, and open to new technologies. In practice, security must result in balancing adequate protection of diverse stakeholders at a reasonable cost. But what does "adequate" and "reasonable" mean?

Again, we must balance the value and risk. A reasonable person would not spend 100,000 euros on a safe to protect 10,000 euros in jewelry. The key question boils down to this: what is the valuation of the assets that need to be protected (the "jewels") and what investment is required to protect them (the "safe")? By putting security and trust on an economic basis, we engage in risk-based reasoning and make rational decisions.

In the future, individuals and enterprises should be able to evaluate risks in terms of quantifiable metrics. Unfortunately, this remains a difficult challenge. We already have metrics about how to develop software securely, but we lack useful metrics for technical security that allow us to evaluate the strengths and weaknesses of a given IT landscape. With better metrics, we could mitigate security risks with insurance, much as we do with other threats like natural disasters. Someday insurers might be able to issue software insurance and cover security losses; at this point, such efforts have failed and it remains an unsolved research challenge.

---

[7] Butler Lampson, "Usable Security: How to Get It," *Communications of the ACM*, Nov. 2009, Vol. 52, No. 11, *http://delivery.acm.org/10.1145/1600000/1592761/ communications200911-dl.pdf?key1=1592761&key2=1340315031&coll=DL&dl= ACM&ip=174.20.74.154&CFID=20574516&CFTOKEN=47500928.*

The major challenges for security economics are twofold. First, we need to put security and risk assessment on a quantitative level. This includes monetary valuation of information representing material and immaterial assets ("what is personal information worth?"), quantitative assessment of risk in Future Internet systems and application landscapes ("what is the potential loss and its probability when consuming this service, using that technology, or pushing this application to the cloud?"), and estimates of the costs of protective measures ("what do I have to invest if I move to a private rather than the public cloud or if I integrate this security service?").

Second, the dynamic nature of the Future Internet obliges us to empower users to constantly monitor and evaluate the threat situation and the security status of their applications and systems. We must support them in taking appropriate action if the circumstances should change. Ideally, a consumer of a service or application could conduct an initial risk assessment, orchestrate security services based on cost/benefit considerations, be alerted to any changes in the situation, and react as appropriate—adding security services, installing security patches, or restricting interactions.

Many of the pieces required to realize this vision are yet to come and deserve further research. Security economics requires a long-term perspective and the interdisciplinary research of computer scientists, economists, and policy makers.

Regulation and Governance

As a critical infrastructure, the Future Internet needs oversight. We already regulate other critical infrastructures like utilities and roads and have international treaties that govern shared resources like the seas and airspace. Similarly, we need new models for governance of the Future Internet.

Who should provide oversight of this future network? Can we leave it to government officials, who may or may not understand what is going on? Should it follow an international model like the UN or European Union? Can we leave governance to corporations that may put profits ahead of public interest, or governments that may put national interests ahead of international fairness?

The WikiLeaks episode demonstrates how powerful interests can shut down an Internet player. Founded in 2006, the international organization publishes documents leaked from government agencies and corporations on the Internet. It came to prominent international attention in 2010 when it began publishing hundreds of thousands of classified US government documents detailing military operations in Afghanistan, Iraq, and diplomatic cables. Not surprisingly, the organization has faced repercussions and legal action from the governments of the United States, Britain, Germany, and other nations. The US Government, Amazon, PayPal, EveryDNS, Visa, and MasterCard all had a hand in trying to shut down WikiLeaks. Regardless of the virtues or merits of WikiLeaks, it is disturbing when private interests in one country can determine whether something lives or dies on the Internet.

If current trends continue, we may see a more fragmented Internet. Countries like China, Russia, or India may decide they don't want to operate under US hegemony and build their own infrastructure. This is not in the interest of a global economy.

Service Delivery Infrastructures: Medieval or Modern Economy?

The Future Internet is often touted as a global phenomenon that will unite diverse participants and bring a more fluid global economy. This is true, but it obscures another danger: the fragmentation of Future Internet platforms into rival camps that discourage free markets and fair competition.

"Today, web services are the shadow of the real economy on the Internet," says Prof. Dr. Max Mühlhäuser, head of the Telecooperation Lab at Technische Universität Darmstadt, Informatics Dept. "Tomorrow, the real economy will be the shadow of the digital economy driven by the Internet of Services."

Software will increasingly become the engine of the modern economy. But it remains unclear how to assure effective governance in this emerging realm. As Prof. Mühlhäuser points out, the Internet of Services is changing so dramatically and rapidly that traditional economic theories,

(continued on next page)

(continued from previous page)

regulatory frameworks, and governance models are too slow and must adapt to this new reality.

One key target for governance is the new platforms of the Future Internet. Prof. Mühlhäuser predicts that service delivery infrastructures (SDIs) will emerge as the new marketplaces of the Internet of Services. At this point, these SDIs are dominated by their creators, and the terms have been designed to their advantage. One example is the monopolistic traits of Apple's App Store as debated, e.g., in the context of the 2010 ban on Adobe Flash. Similarly, other SDIs like Alibaba.com and banking schemes exhibit macroeconomic properties that will be undesirable in the long run. These behaviors run the risk of fragmenting our economy into many economic and digital fiefdoms that Prof. Mühlhäuser calls "medieval markets."

To remedy this situation, governments should take an active interest in the emerging Internet of Services. Prof. Mühlhäuser urges two key steps. First, nations must co-evolve Internet of Services (IoS) approaches, macroeconomic models, and government roles. Second, they must show how software-based macroeconomic governance and SDIs can avoid trusts, monopolies, social injustice, and market fragmentation.

Protection from Cyberwar Attacks

As companies conduct more of their operations on the Internet, they expose themselves to new vulnerabilities. Companies must brace for the threat of cyber attacks.

Cyberwar is often mentioned in the context of national defense. The WikiLeaks episode demonstrates how much damage a non-state actor can do, even to a superpower like the US. In 2010, WikiLeaks published a string of explosive videos and documents hacked from the US government and military. The "Collateral Murder" video showed the massacre of several people on a Baghdad street by an Apache helicopter gunship.

Cyberwar is not only a matter of national security; it also represents a threat to enterprises. For example, when the *Financial Times* quoted the CEO of the US security firm HB Gary Federal as threatening to reveal the identities of hackers associated with WikiLeaks, the hackers turned on him with a vengeance. A shadowy group known as Anonymous hacked into the company account, stole 71,000 emails and put them on the Web for all the world to see (including many embarrassing revelations about the firm's unethical tactics), defaced the CEO's Twitter account, and wiped out all content on his iPad. The CEO was forced to resign and the company and its partners were obliged to publicly disassociate themselves from his tactics. The hackers brought down a firm specializing in information security. This example should serve as a cautionary tale for any enterprise and remind them of their potential vulnerability to a determined and capable cyber foe.

Architectural/Technical Requirements

The architectural and technical requirements are key to the Future Internet's flexibility and longevity. Requirements in this category include scalability, performance, mobility, service orientation, cloud computing, interoperable standards, and routing security.

Scalability

The Future Internet needs to accommodate both a large absolute number of participants (reachable entities) as well as increased traffic volume. Traffic volume will be driven not only by the increased number of users, but more so by increased intense uses of bandwidth, especially video. According to a two-year study of Internet traffic released by Arbor Networks in 2010, video now accounts for up to 75% of overall traffic in the US.

The Future Internet must accommodate large network topologies without demanding exponential increases in operations for the communication network. At this point, scalability poses major barriers. Perhaps the most fundamental issue stems from the routing system: a growing number of autonomous systems, growth of routing tables, and prefix deaggregation for traffic management.

IPv4, with its 32-bit addresses, is running out of address space. The last block of IPv4 addresses was allocated in February 2011. IPv6 will solve the addressing problem for a very long time. IPv4 is a 32-bit protocol that provides 4.3 billion unique addresses. IPv6 is a 128-bit protocol with so many addresses that it is difficult to capture its enormity in written form. It would provide 2^{128} addresses—or about 2^{95} addresses for every person on Earth.

This problem is not new. In the 1990s, Network Address Translation (NAT) became a common technique for aggregating a group of IP addresses onto a single IP address. If NAT had not been implemented, the IPv4 address space would have been exhausted many years ago. Most systems use NAT to enable private networks to access the Internet using a single public IP address. From the outside, all traffic appears to have originated from the gateway machine.

The problem may be solved at a technical level, but the transition is likely to be messy and painful. We have squandered a decade of lead-time in making the transition from IPv4 to IPv6. The problem is nobody wants to move to IPv6. The players have wanted to stay where the crowd is. Early movers have plenty of space, but few people to talk to.

That said, the pain is now severe enough that some are migrating to IPv6. The early movers tend to be have-nots and latecomers who cannot obtain enough address space under the old system, including developing nations in Africa and India.

While NAT was originally used to bring large corporate networks online via a single IP address, now we are seeing countries doing the same. China is a prime example of carrier grade NAT. It has erected an Internet version of the Great Wall, mostly for political control and censorship. Companies must face a world in which large-scale NAT is commonplace. For example, websites may have to share the same address. This has security implications. Some experts have remarked that we are moving toward an "Internet of InterNATs."

Performance: Bandwidth and Latency

There are two aspects to the perceived performance of a given Internet connection: latency and bandwidth. Traditionally, adding more bandwidth to a network to accommodate more traffic has also kept latency constant, or even reduced it, thus improving both throughput and interactive feel.

But there is a downside: growing latency. This is due to the interaction between the increase in buffers (located inside the network in order to be able to realize a given theoretically available bandwidth) and the manner that the workhorse transport protocol of the Internet, TCP/IP, handles traffic overload (called "congestion control"). Over the last few years, this interaction has led to an ever-increasing latency in many areas of the Internet and is starting to impact the usability of interactive applications that rely on speed.

Enterprise software must deal with demands of real time, pervasive computing, sporadic data bursts, and vast numbers of small data units. Twitter is only the beginning of the real-time revolution. The Internet of Things will bring a mega-flood of information: data volumes that double about every 18 months, sometimes requiring very short reaction times to sensor data. All of these challenges need to be addressed by a careful mixture of investing in more infrastructure with higher link speeds and routers and choosing appropriate protocols.

There is a large field of experimentation with alternative methods of congestion control as well as specialized transport protocols such as SCTP or UDT, which try to be smarter about handling lots of small, timely pieces of data (stream control transmission protocol or SCTP) or huge bulk transfer (UDP-based data transfer or UDT). On the inside of the network, an effort called OpenFlow, originally envisioned at the University of California at Berkeley and Stanford University, experiments with new ways of routing packets through the backbones of the Internet without requiring additional hardware. OpenFlow essentially virtualizes the routers so that multiple regimes for packet switching can be in the same physical Internet infrastructure at the same time.

Mobile

Applications must be accessible by and optimized for mobile users on a variety of devices. The number of mobile devices will far outpace tethered devices, so mobility support is a key requirement of the Future Internet.

The original Internet was not designed with mobility in mind. Inevitably, there will be changes in the infrastructure. Due to the rising traffic, mobile networks will be further expanded, and backbone networks will be changed as well. Point-to-point connections will disappear. Telco networks will be part of the Internet infrastructure and be part of the critical infrastructure. Telco infrastructures will be using the Internet in the future, especially routing data packages with IP technology (in fact, some major telcos already have shifted to IP routing in controlled environments). Future requirements include guarantees for data package routing and performance guarantees.

The unique characteristics of mobile devices that roam quickly between different networks pose challenges to existing addressing and naming services of the Internet. TCP/IP is ill suited for such dynamic environments and the large frequency of packet losses can wreak havoc on the performance of mobile connections. Protocols such as SCTP can accommodate rapid changes of IP addresses without interrupting existing connections and are far more tolerant of packet loss than TCP/IP. One could expect adoption of such technologies especially in the mobile realm.

Service Orientation

The vision for the Future Internet is a holistic one in which the network architecture is flexible and adaptable. It must be adaptable to new demands and readily add or delete functionality.

In the future, more and more functionality will be made available as services. This service orientation gives businesses better interoperability, agility, and return on investment. These services should be open to a variety of technologies—traditional ERP environments, cloud, mobile, and so on. Similarly, we need service descriptions that enable web-based services and allow integration of the different machines, such as the devices of the Internet of Things.

The Future Internet should employ the same principles as service-oriented architecture. It should offer services as self-contained "building blocks." Applications should be decoupled from network functionality and services should be loosely coupled and readily accessible by other services and technologies. We must avoid tight coupling of services, infrastructure, and data in order to retain flexibility and control and avoid siloization of information. All these current principles will continue to apply in the Future Internet.

There is a tradeoff to be considered when discussing decoupling. Service orientation can be seen as a "functional" view on software entities. Using services has obvious consequences for scalability and performance. Of equal importance is the consequence for handling data: the functional view normally has the disadvantage that data might be "hidden" behind service interfaces. This makes it difficult to talk about data in a broader sense and data cannot be combined easily in this arrangement.

An alternative trend might be helpful in the Future Internet: a data centric view. In this approach, data is seen as an independent entity that can be used from several services. Many Internet companies collect masses of data from Internet users. Although it is not yet clear how this data can be used, data is becoming more and more important. Some analysts predict "war about data" on the horizon.

Choosing a functional view or a data centric view has consequences for the IT architecture. The Future Internet should offer mechanisms that allow separating data from services. This would avoid data silos and would allow control of data. One idea is to create methods that allow access to data—for example personal data—only for a limited time and a specified purpose.

Cloud Computing

The cloud will play a central role in the Future Internet. Future applications must be optimized for cloud accessibility and deployment. Enterprises must be prepared to operate some, if not all, of their operations in the cloud environment.

The cloud offers well-known benefits such as reducing infrastructure barriers, allowing even small startups to rapidly scale up or down as needed, and shifting IT costs from capital expenses to operational expenses. The cloud can be used to provision a full range of services from data backup to a full suite of enterprise applications. The cloud can be used for multiple roles: Infrastructure as a Service (IAAS), Software as a Service (SaaS), and Platform as a Service (PaaS). Collectively, we can think of the cloud environment as Everything as a Service or *aaS (all of which imply service-oriented architecture).

Yet the cloud also faces a number of barriers. Cloud technologies and models remain a work in progress and are unsuited to many enterprise applications. Cloud offerings are heterogeneous and lack common standards for exchanging data. Many enterprises remain wary because of questions about security, data protection, availability, and service levels.

Enterprises can expect to face many tradeoffs when they move IT into the cloud. Many of the general barriers described in this chapter are particularly troublesome in the cloud. The cloud also poses an array of unique challenges, many of which were outlined in a recent report by a group of experts under the aegis of the Commission of the European Communities, Information Society & Media Directorate-General,[8] and in a recent article in *IEEE Internet Computing*.[9] Here is a brief primer on some major concerns in the cloud environment.

Security

The security question has particular urgency in the cloud. There are many reasons for this, including the lack of physical proximity of data, the lack of acceptable SLAs from cloud providers, and the multitenant environment. Behind the firewall, enterprises feel that they have control of their data. In the cloud, they must trust the provider. The cloud can amplify the scope of malicious use because there is so much data stored in one platform. Many organizations are loath to entrust their sensitive data and reputation to the public cloud.

For small organizations with limited resources, data may be safer in the cloud than on premise. But many organizations feel that public cloud providers don't offer sufficient protection. Most providers find it hard, if not impossible, to meet standards for auditability and to comply with legislation such Sarbanes-Oxley and the Health and Human Services Health Insurance Portability and Accountability Act (HIPAA).

Performance Instability

The cloud is often touted as a solution for organizations with large variations in computing demands. Less well known is the performance variability in cloud implementations themselves.

---

[8] "Opportunities For European Cloud Computing Beyond 2010," Expert Group Report, by the Commission of the European Communities, Information Society & Media Directorate-General, Software & Service Architectures, Infrastructures and Engineering Unit.
http://cordis.europa.eu/fp7/ict/ssai/docs/cloud-report-final.pdf.
[9] Paul Hofmann and Dan Woods, "Cloud Computing: The Limits of Public Clouds for Business Applications," *IEEE Internet Computing*, November/December 2010 (vol. 14 no. 6), *http://www.computer.org/portal/web/csdl/doi/10.1109/MIC.2010.136.*

Researchers in Australia conducted stress tests to demonstrate that Amazon, Google, and Microsoft suffered from variations in performance and availability due to heavy traffic. Specifically, the researchers measured how the cloud providers scaled up and responded to the sudden demand of 2,000 concurrent users. In some cases, response times at different points of the day varied by a factor of 20.[10]

Network Limits and Latency

The applicability cloud model is limited by the speed of transmission. In particular, large data movements are limited by network bandwidth. As applications make more intense use of large volumes of data, data transfer poses an increasing bottleneck. For example, University of California, Berkeley computer scientists calculated the costs of shipping 10 Tbytes of data from the Bay Area to Amazon in Seattle. Given the average bandwidth, sending this data would take 45 days and cost $1,000 in network transfer fees.

In contrast, shipping 10 1-terabyte disks overnight costs only $400. This model of "Netflix for cloud computing" offers a way to avoid some of the latency problems and data transfer costs. In fact, many companies that must transfer massive amounts of data, such as a pharmaceutical company submitting data to the US Food and Drug Administration to win approval for a new drug, often ship whole computers instead of extracting data and sending it over the Internet.

When designing cloud applications, one has to pay close attention to the placement of data. This suggests that the cloud won't be a good option for problems that require instant processing of large amounts of data that must first be sent over the network.

Conversely, given the lack of real-time latency guarantees, the cloud is not suited to uses such as the split-second precision required for stock trading. For this reason, financial service firms often locate their data centers as close as possible to stock exchanges.

---

[10] Brett Winterford, "Stress tests rain on Amazon's cloud," *iTnews,* Aug 20, 2009, *http://www.itnews.com.au/News/153451,stress-tests-rain-on-amazons-cloud.aspx.*

Economic Questions

Enterprises lack proven formulas for the costs and benefits of switching to the cloud. These questions apply to customers (When to switch to the cloud? How costly is migration? Which services are suitable for the cloud and which are not?) and even providers themselves (How much does cloud provisioning cost? What scalability and management support works best? How much quality of service can be guaranteed?). The answers must become clearer as the cloud becomes more popular.

Legal Questions

Cloud providers often combine resources from across the globe and cross international boundaries. In general, many legal Internet issues remain unresolved and the cloud is a case in point. What bodies and laws will regulate essential issues like privacy and security? How will the rights of enterprises and individuals be protected?

Does the Cloud Stifle Innovation?

Some have argued that the cloud model might impair innovation. This argument was presented in a recent article by Paul Hofmann and Dan Woods in *IEEE Internet Computing*.[11] This claim may appear ironic because one of the main attractions of cloud computing is that it frees enterprises from the IT burden and allows them to focus on innovation. This is true—to a point. Hofmann and Woods contend that plain vanilla IT solutions do not allow the kind of customization and fine tuning that can give companies a major competitive advantage from IT. Implemented properly, ERP represents a significant source of competitive advantage, but if ERP becomes a commodity—the cloud model's central premise—it limits a company's ability to innovate.

IT represents a source of competitive advantage for many organizations. In a 2008 *Harvard Business Review* article,[12] Andrew McAfee and Erik Brynjolfsson found that competition within the US economy had acceler-

---

[11] Paul Hofmann and Dan Woods, "Cloud Computing: The Limits of Public Clouds for Business Applications," *IEEE Internet Computing*, November/December 2010 (vol. 14 no. 6), *http://www.computer.org/portal/web/csdl/doi/10.1109/MIC.2010.136*.
[12] Andrew McAfee and Erik Brynjolfsson, "Investing in IT That Makes a Competitive Difference," *Harvard Business Review*, 2008, *www.scribd.com/doc/13415798/Investing-in-IT-That-Makes-a-Competitive-Difference*.

ated to unprecedented levels in the wake of the mainstream adoption of the Internet and commercial enterprise software. The main catalyst was the massive increase in IT power. As the authors write, "A company's unique business processes can now be propagated with much higher fidelity across the organization by embedding it in enterprise information technology. As a result, an innovator with a better way of doing things can scale up with unprecedented speed to dominate an industry."

The average company's IT investment grew from US $3,500 per worker in 1994 to about US $8,000 in 2005. During this period, annual productivity growth in US companies roughly doubled. This period of intensive IT investment ushered in an era of greater turbulence, wider gaps between leaders and laggards, and winner-take-all concentration. The key driver of this trend was that IT enabled improvements in operating models and propagated them quickly and widely. They could deploy powerful technology platforms like ERP, innovate better business processes, and reproduce best practices throughout the enterprise.

But it remains to be seen whether a company can do this with generic cloud IT. Despite all the hype about enabling innovation, the cloud actually impairs the ability of large enterprises to gain competitive advantage because it's optimized for the cloud provider, not the customer. It's designed for ease of maintenance, scalability, and lowest common denominator functionality. It limits the ability of customers to tailor their software and wring real competitive advantage from their IT systems.

Consider Apple. Its shift from a perpetual license model to the iTunes Store's pay-per-use option allowed it to quadruple revenues in four years. The Apple model depends on tight integration between Apple's ERP system and the billing engine, which handles 10 million sales per day. It would be difficult, if not impossible, to set up such a tight integration between the cloud's ERP and Apple's highly proprietary billing software.

What do all these concerns mean for the future of the cloud model? The cloud is a new paradigm with advantages and disadvantages. Over time, some of these concerns will be solved or the risks will be reduced to acceptable levels. For now, these concerns have kept cloud adoption at a modest pace. According to IDC, less than 10% of worldwide IT spending will be used on cloud computing by 2013 *(www.slideshare.net/JorFigOr/ cloud-computing-2010-an-idc-update)*.

For most organizations, the question of whether to move into the cloud will be a matter of weighing pros and cons. There's a "sweet spot" for cloud business applications where the trade-off is optimum—and at this point, that spot is around HR and CRM. As we might expect, this is where we also see the most common SaaS applications, such as CRM and HR applications without too much functionality or customization.

We also are likely to see virtualization outside the public cloud. Some companies might establish private clouds, which provide benefits like economies of scale without the drawbacks of a public cloud.

Cloud Scalability

The cloud is often touted as an infinitely scalable resource. In fact, the cloud poses its own scalability problems. Generally speaking, cloud code and data are not structured for efficient scaling. Most cloud systems achieve scalability through horizontal replication rather than actually increasing the availability of necessary segments or increasing the resources for specific tasks. Data size and diversity grows, but current cloud systems are typically restricted either to small data sets that can be easily replicated or large data sets that are only read. Generally, they offer little support for update-intensive applications or advanced analytic capabilities.

Most business applications today rely on consistent transactions supported by relational databases, which unfortunately do not scale. The early clouds lacked a scalable storage with an API as rich as SQL.

High-volume, mission-critical transactional systems face major challenges in the cloud. Scalable storage with a SQL-like API remains an unsolved research problem. There cannot be a completely general solution for applications that rely on consistent transactions in the old way in a truly distributed environment, due to the so called CAP Theorem. The CAP Theorem basically states that you can only solve any two out of the three problems of consistency, availability, and partition tolerance.

Rather than trying to solve the impossible general problem, cloud providers have devised their own proprietary solutions. Amazon Dynamo, Facebook Cassandra, and Google Big Table each rely on much simpler key value stores (where data is stored without SQL schemas), sometimes sacrificing consistency, sometimes expressiveness. These methods can be scalable but often don't allow storage of complex structures like relational databases do. Consequently, these solutions lack the power required for many business applications.

Interoperable Standards

Standards provide a basis for interaction; the Internet itself would not have existed without the widespread adoption of standards for routing, transport, naming, and the like (BGP, TCP/IP, DNS). Similar standardization needs to exist for the Future Internet's higher levels of functionality. TEXO made an important step forward with its work on the development of the Unified Service Description Language (USDL), now being pursued by the W3C (described in more detail later in this chapter).

Interoperability becomes increasingly important as more operations shift to the cloud. Unfortunately, cloud providers speak different languages. All the major providers offer unique, and often proprietary, data storage (for example, Google's BigTable, Amazon's Dynamo, and Facebook's Cassandra). Scalable data storage isn't an interchangeable commodity and is unlikely to be for a long time. As described later in this section, scalable relational database management systems remain an unsolved scientific problem, posing huge challenges for interoperability. Transporting data between different cloud providers remains a major stumbling block. As long as cloud providers speak different languages, data storage will not be an interchangeable commodity.

The cloud hasn't yet gone through standardization efforts like the software industry. Customers cannot easily move data from one cloud to another. For example, a customer might have to upload his contact data from SalesForce, transport it to Google's AppEngine, and convert it into another format for Google contacts. Cloud users can face severe constraints in moving their data from one cloud provider to another and find themselves locked in. At this point, enterprises have few options for middleware to enable them to fly freely from cloud to cloud.

Although some basic agreement on standards is essential, the idea of universal standards is a pipe dream. Innovation will always produce new standards for specialized purposes. We are unlikely to see a holistic Future Internet with common protocols. A more realistic objective is *interoperability*. The Future Internet will have to embrace heterogeneous technologies, but interoperability remains a major challenge.

Most likely, the Future Internet will show "emergent standards." This term covers what is already visible in the Internet. The Future Internet will become an even bigger experimental field for doing business and, as a consequence, a source of emerging standards. One requirement will be proving support for communities to develop appropriate standards for their domain.

Routing Security

Routing remains vulnerable in the current Internet and needs better security.

Routing is easily hijacked or blocked, as we saw in the previous chapter. Moreover, the number of prefixes, or IP address blocks, is becoming increasingly difficult to manage. Over the last five years it has more than doubled and stood at 350,000 by the end of 2010. The number of routing table entries is predicted to hit 2 million in the next decade, according to *Security Week*.

The Border Gateway Protocol (BGP) directs IP packets to their correct destination network. BGP tables contain all active network prefixes. In practice, however, the Internet is a collection of autonomous systems routing domains that often forward information without verification—a process known as "routing by rumor." These autonomous systems decide, sometimes arbitrarily, whether to trust routing information and are easily fooled.

Some efforts are underway to make routing more secure. The Internet Engineering Task Force (IETF) has initiated a working group that is working on a Resource Public Key Infrastructure (RPKI) that provides authorization for who can originate a route to an address.

The depletion of IPv4 addresses further complicates this issue. IPv6 will introduce billions of additional addresses and the transition from IPv4 to IPv6 may actually exacerbate the problem because the two protocols will have to coexist for years.

Routing table expansion remains a pressing problem for the entire Internet community. Legacy appliances cannot handle newer protocols like IPv6 and DNSSEC. We need new standards, practices for scalable routing, and replacement of aging hardware.

Business Requirements

Ultimately, business drives interest in the Internet. Requirements in this area include business network orchestration, ease of orchestration, service description and semantics, service level agreements, new billing modules, energy efficiency, and collaboration.

Business Network Orchestration

The Future Internet must facilitate the formation and operation of business networks. This is a key to economic agility, remaining competitive and innovating new business models.

Business networks form to address needs and opportunities that are best addressed by networks rather than single parties. Ideally, they create higher net value, competitive advantage, and new opportunities for all participants, stakeholders, and customers. These business networks run the gamut from highly structured to loosely defined, centrally coordinated to peer-to-peer. Examples include logistics networks, smart electricity grids and energy marketplaces.

Business network orchestration leverages IT to facilitate the arrangement, coordination, and management of business networks. The members need a platform and mechanisms that allow them to span many barriers including geography, time, capabilities, government jurisdictions, and so on. They must design, run, analyze, continuously refine, and eventually terminate the value chain. They must combine a series of interconnected businesses, business processes, and relationships with business networks—all while managing a continuous flow of material goods, information, people, services, finances, rights, and ownership.

Ideally, integration of business networks should be easy, quick, and seamless. Creating enterprise networks will be as easy as creating social networks. The vision of the virtual enterprise—a term coined two decades ago—may finally come to pass.

Ease of Orchestration

Business network orchestration involves a number of key phases, including negotiation, establishment, enactment, monitoring, and termination of the network.

Taking a historical perspective, we can see that orchestration—whether it be Kanban, business process reengineering, or Six Sigma—usually represents an effort to establish order amid chaos. In the past, most of these approaches have required significant preparation before they can be implemented and produce results. The prep time can be measured in months or even years.

Such sluggish timescales are no longer practical in today's world. The business web must accelerate each phase of the orchestration lifecycle. These phases should be enabled in minutes or hours. The ever-faster speed of IT renders complex calculations in fractions of seconds. If SAP HANA can process billions of records in less than a second, then the orchestration lifecycle must adhere to similar timescales.

Part of the solution depends on legal agreements and negotiations between the business partners. Today the App Store has set a new standard and model for business. In addition to Apple, big IT players such as Amazon, Google, and SAP are moving toward their own versions of app stores. But these legal agreements remain unwieldy. For example, the Apple App Store for iOS and Mac uses only standard agreements drawn up by Apple, leaving app developers with only two options: take it or leave it. The enactment phase takes one to four weeks before a newly developed app is available for purchase on the store.

The Future Internet will demand more practical, flexible, and business-friendly approaches. Business web orchestration will entail negotiations between relatively equal partners. They must be enacted more quickly. In short, they depend on ease of orchestration.

Business network orchestration must facilitate each key phase. Here is a summary of the key tasks:

- **Negotiation:** The negotiation phase must be structured to allow ad hoc interaction among stakeholders. Business partners need mechanisms to capture information, preserve it, replay it, and prepare it for further electronic processing. They need processes to agree on marketplace mechanisms and remuneration models

- **Establishment:** The clouds can facilitate business network orchestration and relieve the participants from installing their own specialized IT systems for new business networks. They also can take advantage of other prepackaged building blocks such as business process model fragments or technologies for specific markets

- **Enactment:** This phase marks the beginning of collaborations. Process models and transactions take place. Exceptions need to be managed

- **Monitoring:** Monitoring is an ongoing function that involves all the other phases. It operates in parallel to the negotiations, establishment, enactment, and termination phases. Partners need the ability to monitor and analyze the collaborative processes and transactions. They need the capability to identify resource shortages and bottlenecks

- **Termination:** Even the most successful business network inevitably reaches its end. Enterprises need mechanisms to terminate individual partners, hand off to new partners, or dissolve the entire network

Service Description and Semantics

Service discovery is crucial for business webs. This requires better methods of service description and discovery. Current techniques are based on keyword, metadata, and ontology-based search. This approach is suitable within enclosed domains but is less viable in open domains because the Internet of Services is simply too vast and heterogeneous. This places the onus on consumers to know what they want before they search, limiting the exploitation of the full potential of the Internet of Services.

The Future Internet demands a better paradigm for discovery and description of services. The THESEUS project is pursuing some of these goals. One effort is the creation of Unified Service Description Language (USDL). USDL was developed as a platform-neutral, scalable language for describing services and enabling them to be more easily commercialized online. USDL is adaptable to new concepts and can be configured to meet the requirements of specific applications and industries. They include professional, transactional, informational, software, digital media, platform, and infrastructure services. As it now stands, there are myriad service description efforts on many fronts: service-oriented architecture, semantic web services, SaaS, cloud computing, business process outsourcing, and economic value. USDL seeks to wrap all these elements into a single package. SAP Research has played a lead role in developing this standard as part of the TEXO project within the THESEUS research program.

Service Level Agreements and Quality of Service Guarantees

A panoply of offerings exist without service-level agreements (SLAs) or quality of service guarantees. For example, at this point, cloud providers offer precious few service guarantees, forcing customers to shoulder most of the risks. Cloud providers compete to offer the lowest possible price, which militates against better service guarantees for performance, privacy, and security. Cloud providers could offer better security and privacy but are discouraged from doing so because they may price themselves out of the market. "Things like this have their price," said Prof. Dr. Oliver Günther, Dean of the School of Business and Economics and a professor of Information Systems at Humboldt-Universität in Berlin. "It's important to make service characteristics transparent so that people can react accordingly and buy not only the kind of services they want but also the levels of privacy, security, and performance that they need."

At this point, enterprises have few guarantees. What's the guaranteed uptime? What are the repercussions if the provider fails to meet these standards? What happens to customer data if the company moves to a different provider?

Cloud providers offer precious few protections to enterprises that trust all their IT to the cloud. In the article, "Why Cloud Computing Will Never Be Free," Dave Durkee points out that "pricing pressure results in a commoditization of cloud services that deemphasizes enterprise requirements such as guaranteed levels of performance, uptime, and vendor responsiveness."[13]

---

[13] Dave Durkee, "Why Cloud Computing Will Never Be Free," *Communications of the ACM,* Vol. 53 No. 5, Pages 62–69, 2010, *http://cacm.acm.org/magazines/2010/5/87259-why-cloud-computing-will-never-be-free/fulltext.*

In one typical example, one major cloud provider guarantees an availability level of 99.999% uptime, or no more than five minutes of downtime a year. If it fails to meet this standard, it gives a 10% discount on its charges for any month in which that level of availability is not achieved. As Durkee notes, "If a customer really needs five-nines of uptime, a 10% discount is not going to even come close to the cost of lost revenue, breach of end-user service levels, or loss of market share due to credibility issues."

The lack of enterprise-grade SLAs in the cloud is amplified when customers rely on multiple cloud providers that offer different levels of guarantees. What service does a user receive when cloud provider X offers SLA 1 and provider Y offers SLA 2? To date, there is no technical solution to the problem of federated SLAs.

New Models for Billing and Metering

We also need new models for billing to reflect the micro-services of the Future Internet. For example, an international business executive who relies on an iPad might pay roaming charges 100 times higher than the rates at home. The roaming pricing model is not suitable for the next generation of the Internet.

The Future Internet opens up possibilities for new revenue mechanisms and price models such as real-time pricing, incentive-based pricing, trust-based pricing, and geographic-specific pricing—all integrated into the service offerings.

Energy Efficiency

In the future, application developers must put more emphasis on energy efficiency. Information and communications technology (ICT) energy consumption is unsustainable. Today ICT consumes about 2% of energy usage worldwide (and thus accounts for an equal percentage of CO_2 emissions). Of this, data centers represent nearly one quarter of ICT energy consumption. These power demands may continue to increase with the emergence of more automation and powerful applications.

Another new burden on energy requirements is the devices of the Internet of Things. These are typically small devices run on batteries, but their sheer numbers will create a major burden on power demands.

Data volume on the networks increases by a factor of 10 approximately every five years. This amounts to an increase of 16 to 20% per year. These increases in power demands are not sustainable and thus we need greater efficiency and greener technologies.[14]

Fortunately, the Future Internet also holds great promise in providing technologies to reduce energy consumption. For example, smart traffic control systems could reduce urban traffic congestion and optimize traffic flow, thus reducing vehicle exhaust.[15]

Collaborative Platforms

Web 2.0 and the consumer space have clearly demonstrated the value of collaboration and social networking. These technologies found their way into the enterprise through the back door; in the future, they must be integrated into enterprise IT. Enterprise software must provide more than just the sharing of content; it must facilitate collaboration. It must be designed to foster user-generated content and co-creation.

One requirement for the Future Internet is to provide basic tools for collaboration. This is especially important for software development processes. The tools should enable "instantaneous collaboration" between developers, both synchronously and asynchronously. The tools should use the context of the knowledge workers, the communication should take his current situation into consideration. Tools should include telco services.

Software Development Requirements

Software development requirements for the Future Internet include ease of participation, business app creation, faster development cycles, and the concept of timeless software.

---

[14] "Future Internet Strategic Research Agenda," by Future Internet X-ETP Group, Pierre-Yves Danet 2010, *http://www.future-internet.eu/fileadmin/documents/ reports/FI-SRA-V1_1_final_clean_050210.pdf.*
[15] "Future Internet: The Cross-ETP Vision Document," Dimitri Papadimitriou (editor), 2009, *http://www.nessi-europe.com/files/PositionPapers/ETP%20Vision%20 on%20Future%20Internet.pdf.*

Ease of Participation

New protocols and new applications should offer ease of participation, similar to the way that cloud and Internet applications can be consumed more easily than on-premise solutions can today.

The ability to onboard new suppliers and create ad hoc value chains must become easier to enable broader and more spontaneous participation in commerce.

New protocols must be designed to make configuration easy or to auto-configure by default. Representational State Transfer (REST) provides an example of a protocol designed for easy consumption using existing infrastructure.

Programming Models and Resource Control

Current programming models offer little support for horizontal and vertical scalability, especially in large heterogeneous environments. New programming models need to allow programmers to reason about their application designs and their deployment on the cloud without unduly exposing the underlying complexity. The model must support manageability of the devised applications and services in a way that allows efficient controlling over distribution and enforcing of resource consumption restrictions on the system side.

Systems Development and Systems Management

The cloud relies on heavy automation of system administration. Inevitably, software development needs to directly target such automated environments, cutting out human intermediaries such as system administrators. We must create automated, intelligent systems capable of balancing requirements and capabilities. We also need new methods of describing services and managing dynamic composition and other activities.

Business App Creation

The Future Internet platform must facilitate the development of new applications. This is not simply a matter of reprovisioning classical applications such as ERP, but enabling the creation of new applications, even those we cannot yet anticipate. This is the essence of the business web. Research initiatives that are creating next generation applications provide hints of what could be possible on the Future Internet.

Faster Development Cycles

Software developers can no longer assume a two- or three-year development cycle. They must think in terms of weeks and months, not years.

Requirements for faster development cycles include:

- A cloud-centric development platform

- A collaborative development environment: Users need to be integrated early in the development process such as in the "design thinking" approach

- Continuous platform and application monitoring and analytics: Developers should monitor which features are being used and quality of experience. This feedback enables them to fine tune applications accordingly

- Continuous evolution (end-to-end closed loop): The Future Internet should be an enabler for creative software development by providing a construction set that people can use for developing their own creative applications. These applications need not be major ones. Applications will start smaller in the Future Internet. You would start small with an application and enhance it step by step

- Social Software Engineering: The Future Internet should provide tools for an easy, context-driven collaboration between software developers

Timeless Software

In the future, large-scale, enterprise software must adapt to change while delivering continuity and reliability at low cost. At SAP, this mandate has found expression in the notion of "timeless software"—or software that is architected on principles of fast integration of emerging technologies. This idea applies well beyond SAP and provides a useful framework for approaching the Future Internet in general. The Future

Internet will mix a variety of elements including on-premise solutions, clouds, services, devices, and new solutions. Technological progress will become less about periodic replacement and more about constant adaptation and evolution.

The idea of timeless software has been championed by SAP CTO Vishal Sikka. He illustrates this concept with the analogy of the Boeing 747 jetliner. The plane was first released in the 1960s and today, more than 40 years later, it continues to fly the skies around the world. In an era when product lifespans are increasingly compressed, this airplane continues to fly as a mainstay of commercial aviation. Of course, the airframe has been updated with modern technology like newer engines, navigation systems, cockpits, interiors, and so on. But the basic design still follows the fundamental principles envisioned nearly half a century ago.

Enterprise software follows a similar model. The basic framework remains constant and allows the components to be continuously renovated to keep pace with technological improvements. As Sikka says, "It continuously evolves in a constant cycle of renovation."

Software providers must offer software that allows evolution without disruption or excessive costs. They must provide full-spectrum functionality yet remain adaptable to new technologies that enhance that functionality. This includes offerings that make use of the Future Internet. The airplane is a single entity with a clear border. But enterprise software in the Future Internet will be using resources from the Internet, diminishing this clear border. Lifecycle management becomes all-important.

Large-scale software faces continuous change over its lifetime. According to Sikka, this poses several key challenges for next generation products. Developers must build applications that serve a diverse, globally distributed body of customers and that are efficient and coherent and are adaptable to technological evolution.

The next enterprise programming model must:

- Enable developers across many domains and specializations to use their native abstractions and conveniences

- Support a family of integrated domain-specific languages and tooling conveniences to build software artifacts with maximum efficiency and productivity

- Allow extensions in many different ways

- Be ready to integrate new languages

- Be able to be renovated and embedded in other programming
  models

Enterprises—software developers in particular—must put lifecycle
management in the forefront of their thinking. "Just as every few years
we humans shed most of our cells, acquire new memories, lessons, decisions, and beliefs, evolve and yet stay essentially who we are," writes
Sikka, "I believe it is possible for software to renovate itself completely
and yet continuously."

Ideally, the Future Internet should help companies to achieve this
and provide means for renovating, replacing parts of enterprise software
in a coherent way.

Putting the Pieces Together

The Future Internet represents a complicated puzzle. It represents
a diverse array of complex technical, economic, and social questions.
As we have seen, the solutions are not always clear. Whatever the final
outcome, the good news is that the end result will arm enterprises with
a more complete menu of options. With this new toolbox, they will be
better positioned to run more efficiently, make new innovations, and
develop novel business models. We now turn to the next frontier: the
business models of the Future Internet.

The Future Internet: New Business Models

and Affected Industries

The Future Internet will be a disruptive phenomenon—and new business models will be the knife edge of that disruption. The technology itself won't be the main paradigm shift; rather it will be the new innovations and processes that make use of the technology.

The Internet already has spawned a boom in business models. Indeed, the Internet has disrupted virtually every industry and allowed companies to move existing services online, offer new ones, and gain new efficiencies. It has given birth to new companies and entirely new industries. In the Future Internet, the business model will once again be a key to success.

This chapter explores how the Future Internet and business webs will give rise to new business models, and how enterprises can be smarter in creating and analyzing these new models. As we saw in Chapter 2, there are many significant barriers on the road to the Future Internet. As these problems are solved, the Future Internet will create a new environment—and businesses must be prepared for it. This chapter will cover:

- Why business models are the real payoff of the Future Internet and why process innovations are generally more profitable than technical ones

- How to use IT for strategic advantage

- How to analyze potential business models

- Examples of potential new business models made possible by the Future Internet

The Future Internet will be a disruptive force that takes advantage of exponential progress in key areas such as the growth of computer power (for example, Moore's Law, which holds that the number of transistors that can be placed inexpensively on an integrated circuit doubles every two years) and the value of networks (such as Metcalf's Law, which states that the value of a telecommunications network is proportional to the square of the number of connected users). As a result, there are opportunities for new business models that would have been impossible only a few years ago.

Consider the iPod. Today the iPod is a ubiquitous device. As of September 2010, Apple had sold 275 million of the devices. The computational power of a $200 iPod would have cost $1 billion dollars in 1976. New technology enabled a business model that would have been impossible a few years earlier. But the larger story is not the computational power of the device but the innovation of a killer business model that displaced industry incumbents. Apple accomplished this by cleverly applying the capabilities of the Internet, namely effortless dissemination of information to an existing supply chain, exchanging the traditional controlling factor (ownership of the physical record factories and physical record stores) with a new digital rights management system (DRM) embedded in their devices. The business model relied on the DRM embedded in the iPod hardware and its closed system. By creating a new business model, it created a workable business model for downloading music, a feat that had eluded the music industry for years. Apple collected three major pieces into one chain: music, distribution, and retailing. (Business model innovation is not necessarily a matter of creating entirely new models; rather it often is a matter of combining multiple business models of the existing world. This could be a matter of aggregating old models and roles into one chain, or aggregating the functions and cutting out the middlemen.) This completely changed the game for the music industry and Apple itself. Before the launch of the iPod and iTunes store, Apple had been a struggling company. Within a decade, Apple's combination of product innovation and business model innovation created a market approximately 30 times larger than its original one.[16]

The challenge is to identify and refine novel business models that turn technology into useful services and revenue. How can we create and evaluate promising business models? Can we find an analytical framework to evaluate business models amid the uncertainty of the Future Internet? Do we need new economic theories to guide us in the Future Internet? How can business models of existing Web-based service industries be migrated to the Future Internet?

New Services and New Business Models

Information technology already has enabled companies to decompose large systems and business processes and replace them with ever more fine-grained services. In the Future Internet these services could become components that can be utilized in many ways: outsourced, insourced, repeatedly resold externally, automated, and so on.

If we can bring these capabilities to reality, the Future Internet is likely to create a boom in small services and businesses. These microbusinesses will become the basis of more granular and composable business models.

---

[16] Zhenya Lindgardt, Martin Reeves, George Stalk, and Martin S. Deimler, "Business Model Innovation: When the Game Gets Tough, Change the Game," Boston Consulting Group, (2009), *http://www.bcg.com/documents/file36456.pdf.*

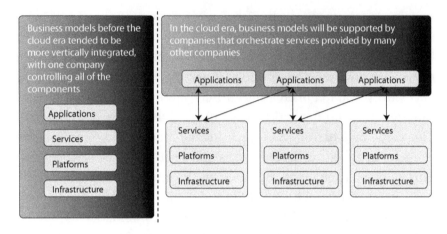

Figure 3-1. How Business Models Are Changing in the Cloud Era

The Future Internet will make it easier to spontaneously form value chains that combine diverse participants, adaptable deployment models, delivery channels, and, of course, new business models. The Future Internet will be characterized by co-creation of value: it will be a flexible platform that unites people in collective value generation.

If services are exposed and accessible, new niches open and partners can derive greater value from their services and solutions. Better service descriptions, such as the Unified Service Description Language (USDL), will encourage the creation of new services by enabling the discovery and acquisition of component services from others.

Clouds will provide a vital element in these new business models of the Future Internet. By making computation, storage, and applications flexibly available, the cloud will spawn a huge array of services and facilitate fast and easy composition of these services into higher-level services. This may be labeled as "Composite as a Service." Ubiquitous access to application functionality will encourage the formation of collaborative networks between partners and cross-partner business processes.

As these services become cheaper, more plentiful, and mature, enterprises will no longer be able to find competitive advantage with just their internal IT departments. Enterprises will be able to distinguish themselves and gain competitive advantage by forming partner networks.

One key task will be orchestrating these services. This requires "choreography technology" for managing cross-partner business processes. One effect of the cloud revolution will be to increase the role of Business Process Management (BPM) technology.

Business Models: The Real Payoff of the Future Internet

Dr. Martin Curley, Director of Intel Labs Europe, is a leading world authority on business model innovation. He is the coauthor of *Managing IT Innovation for Business Value* (Intel Press, 2007) and *Knowledge Driven Entrepreneurship* (Springer, 2010), as well as numerous journal articles. Much of Dr. Curley's work explores the relationship between IT, innovation, and business models.

According to Dr. Curley, business model innovation is likely to be one of the most profitable outcomes of the Future Internet. Knowledge-driven business will grow ever more important and the Future Internet will provide the platform. It will accelerate and amplify business model innovation by making it easier to form and diffuse new models. He believes that this explosion of the knowledge economy will unleash a wave of innovation that is unprecedented in human history.

First, let us step back and examine where innovation really comes from. Dr. Curley cites the Doblin group's ten types of innovation taxonomy that groups innovations in four focus areas as a holistic way of looking at innovation:

- Finance (business model, networking)

- Process (enabling processes, core processes)

- Offering (product performance, product system, service)

- Delivery (channel, brand, customer experience)

Many people have a misperception about the true dynamics of innovation, especially the investment and returns on innovation. They wrongly assume that innovation is typically a new "wow" product. In fact, a sober analysis of the data shows that the most profitable innovation tends to occur in less glamorous, behind-the-scenes business processes.

Doblin Analysis studied the volume of innovation efforts for the last ten years and discovered that they were most common in product performance and product systems. In other words, most companies focus on the offering—the new widget that they hope will earn millions.

But it's a different story when it comes to returns on these innovations. According to Doblin Analysis, the highest returns come from innovations in business models and ecosystems. Over ten years of innovation, the largest cumulative value creation has come from financial innovations. Ironically, product performance actually has the lowest returns.

In other words, business model innovation turns out to be more profitable than product innovation. Apple is perhaps the most obvious example of how a company has disrupted its industry with a new business process. As discussed previously, Apple hasn't succeeded because it invented new technology (the iPod was a repackaging of existing technology with a highly attractive and usable user interface); rather Apple succeeded because it created a more efficient and appealing model for that technology. Apple engineered a complete end-to-end business model from content providers to consumers, leaving incumbent players high and dry. Dr. Curley predicts that such disruptive innovations will become more common with the Future Internet and they will leverage the network effect to diffuse very quickly, particularly in the case of service innovations. According to him, business model innovation is "the core of profitability."

This is why business webs represent such a powerful opportunity. The Future Internet and business webs promise to help businesses exploit opportunities more adroitly. They will be able to combine services and quickly construct new business models.

Knowledge-Driven Entrepreneurship

Business model innovation goes hand-in-hand with broader economic trends. In the future, knowledge-driven business services will expand to a greater percentage of our economy. The Future Internet will be *the* platform for knowledge-driven entrepreneurship. Dr. Curley predicts that "knowledgeification" (a concept and term coined by Gene Meieran of Intel) will accelerate innovation much as electrification did in the previous century.

Dr. Curley believes that Future Internet platforms will spur innovation in two main ways: the *emergence* of new ideas, processes, and business models, and the *convergence* of thinking and collaboration that leads to new innovation.

Drawing on the work of several academics, Dr. Curley outlined the principles of knowledge dynamics.

First, knowledge multiplies when shared, unlike other goods. Most materials are like cookies: if one person takes a bite, there's less for everybody else. "Most physical goods are rival goods," Dr. Curley says. "If you share them, you actually lose them or they become smaller." Knowledge follows a different pattern: it's like a cookie that actually gets bigger whenever somebody takes a bite. Knowledge is a non-rival good.

Second, value is created when knowledge moves from point of origin to point of need. A knowledgeable mechanic creates value when he fixes a broken car.

Third, mutual leverage provides the optimal utilization of resources.

These laws are important because we are beginning the century of revolutionary gains in knowledge. In the 20th century, electrification was a key innovation. The movement of electrons—facilitated by infrastructure like utilities and grids—powered most of the innovations of the century.

"Knowledgeification is going to be what powers the major innovations of the 21st century," said Dr. Curley. "And what we will need is significant infrastructure and standards."

Laws of Knowledge Dynamics

1. Knowledge multiplies when shared
2. Innovation value is created when knowledge moves from point of origin to point of need
3. Collaboration for mutual leverage provides the optimal utilization of resources, both tangible and intangible

Source: Debra M. Amidon, Piero Formica

This revolution requires a new information network. Enter the Future Internet. "These developments depend on delivery of cheap knowledge on demand—'knowledgeification.' It will deliver value at an affordable price and generate huge gains in global wealth and quality of life."

A business model describes the rationale of how an organization creates, delivers, and captures value. The model serves as the glue that connects the overall strategy to the business processes. More and more of these processes are moving online with the Future Internet.

The Future Internet, says Dr. Curley, will accelerate the implementation of business model innovations and the diffusion of business capability and value. Business model innovation involves two phases: creation and diffusion/adoption.

Again, people often have a misperception about business models. They often assume that business model *creation* is the key step; in fact, says Dr. Curley, the *diffusion* and adoption of the components that underpin these models are more important. As the old saying goes, genius is 1% inspiration and 99% perspiration. For every person with an idea, it takes 99 to execute that idea. Dr. Curley says that "innovation is thus a team sport."

The Future Internet will help on both counts. It will make it easier to form new models and diffuse them. The Future Internet gives us a more powerful platform for partnerships and collaboration. According to Dr. Curley and others such as the European Internet Foundation, mass collaboration will become a dominant paradigm of the future. "If we build it, we're going to unleash a new wave of innovation that's probably unprecedented in the history of mankind," he said. "We have the opportunity globally to create a new platform for knowledge-driven entrepreneurship, which will allow both business and mankind to progress at a rate faster than ever before. We are entering a third wave of the impact of computing, where mass connectivity is enabling the power of collective societal intelligence."

Managing the Complexity

According to Dr. Curley, the Future Internet will be an infrastructure and could possibly become the societal operating system for the entire planet. A corporate IT department represents a microcosm for some of the broader challenges that lie ahead. A corporate IT department must contend with warring factions, governance, security, and heterogeneous elements. As such, the corporate IT department represents an "intra-Internet" and may provide an analogy that helps us think about how to approach the Future Internet as a whole.

What are the factors that enable enterprises to use their technology to advance their business goals? How can enterprises address the complexity of opportunity in the Future Internet? How can we create models to approach these new opportunities? How can people like product managers, technology vendors, entrepreneurs, and government officials begin to address the Future Internet?

One way to approach the puzzle is to begin with the needs of society. What social needs are currently not being met? What is the public demanding? What are the existing technologies and capabilities of your organization? How do these two map to each other? Once we overlay the technological capabilities with the needs of society, we can begin to spot new opportunities.

After addressing such questions of vision and strategy, enterprises should turn to the questions of business models and processes.

Using IT for Strategic Advantage

The Future Internet comes with a mandate: enterprises must become more analytical in scrutinizing potential IT investments and business models.

IT is becoming an ever-more vital source of innovation and strategic advantage. As Dr. Curley points out, business process innovation is the core of profitability. IT is a key element of both implementing and improving business processes. IT innovation helps assemble new, emerging, and existing technology and knowledge into business solutions.

Dr. Curley cites a study that reported the results of an Accenture survey of 450 companies. Improvements in *core processes* returned 2–3% improvements—certainly worthwhile but not a game-changer. Investments that optimized *existing processes* returned 10–15% cost savings, a more significant improvement in back-end efficiency. But the real payoff came in the processes that transformed the enterprise with new capabilities. Projects that transformed the enterprise with *new capabilities* returned ten times the initial investment.[17]

Information Technology is an unusual resource that delivers more capability at lower cost each year. Today we take Moore's Law for granted and sometimes forget just how revolutionary technological progress really is. Consider this comparison cited by Dr. Curley. In 1978, a commercial flight from New York to Paris took eight hours and cost approximately 900 euros. Today the flight time and cost remain about the same. If aircraft technology improved at the rate of Moore's Law, the flight would be completed in one second and cost half a cent! Obviously, such improvement remains as farfetched as Star Trek-style beaming a person to a distant destination. In IT, however, such improvements are not only attainable but a trend that has remained constant for decades. Therefore, IT investment should be a priority for two reasons: the potential returns on the investment are unusually high and so is the rate of obsolescence of old technology.

IT is a major driver of economic growth. IT allows enterprises to automate more processes, lower costs, reach into new markets, and use assets more efficiently. IT produces value in several ways including:

- Automating and optimizing existing processes for incremental improvements in productivity, speed, or quality

- Reengineering core processes for improvements in productivity and efficiency

- Transforming the enterprise with new processes and organizational capabilities to drive new growth

- Embedding IT in products and service offerings to provide a better, higher-value product or service

- Providing better information to enable better and faster decision making

---

[17] Martin Curley, *Managing Information Technology for Business Value: Practical Strategies for IT and Business Managers,* Intel Press (2007).

In general, most enterprises recognize that IT can produce strategic advantage. But according to Dr. Curley, most have only a vague notion of how to do this. This lack of clarity poses a major impediment. IT organizations are partnering with business units and expected to produce competitive advantage for the company. If companies could gain a more accurate picture of their IT investments, they could make better investments, optimize IT value, and gain greater competitive advantage. According to Dr. Curley, the key is to deploy IT in a systematic way that delivers ongoing value.

Analyzing Potential Models

Unfortunately, enterprises often lack methodologies for analyzing the benefits of IT. Traditionally, the business value of IT has been loosely defined. Nowadays, enterprises need more specific evidence, metrics, and return on investment (ROI).

In navigating the Future Internet, enterprises must take a more systematic approach to IT investments. Dr. Curley urges them to adopt a more disciplined, analytical approach such as the IT Capability Maturity Framework and Model. He was inspired by the idea of Capability Maturity Models developed by researchers at Carnegie Mellon and developed a Capability Maturity Framework that was applicable to business IT.

First, enterprises must examine their own IT structures within a Capability Maturity Framework. The goal is to assess the level of maturity of these processes and the outcomes that they deliver. Any IT structure can be classified into one of five categories or levels of maturity: ad hoc, repeatable, defined, managed, or optimized.

The IT Capability Maturity Framework consists of four basic macro processes and strategies, which should be aligned with overall business strategies and context. Here is a brief synopsis of each:

- **Manage for IT business value:** IT investments should be viewed as a means to maximize overall business benefits such as profitability and growth. IT should not be viewed as a purely technical investment, but one with broad benefits for the entire enterprise. As Dr. Curley notes, it is very hard to deliver high IT value at low costs. A business really has no choice but continuous investment in IT. As the old saying goes, you must spend money to make money.

- **Manage the IT budget:** Enterprises should seek continuous cost reduction and shift funds from low-yield investments to high-yield investments that bring competitive advantage. They should decommission old technology and look for cheaper ways to deliver the same services. Many organizations are saddled with what Dr. Curley calls "investment inertia." They devote most of their IT budget to maintaining the status quo and allot only a small portion for strategic innovations.

- **Manage the IT capability:** Ongoing management of IT capability is a key to sustainable competitive advantage—and this demands a systematic approach.

As Dr. Curley says, "Sustainable competitive advantage from IT comes not from individual 'stovepipe' solutions, but from an IT capability that is very effective in delivering new strategic applications and delivering them faster and better than competing companies."[18]

Some organizations take an approach of viewing IT projects like financial options. For example, Intel uses a Business Value Index to assess the potential value of future IT investments. The methodology assesses the attractiveness of an investment along three vectors: business value, IT efficiency, and financial attractiveness. This allows an organization to track an IT project as it moves through the stages of concept, requirements, prototyping, development, and so on. The project then can be "stage gated," that is, funded in stages, contingent on meeting certain criteria.

- **Manage IT like a business:** According to Dr. Curley, IT should be run like any other successful business. Business units should be treated like customers and IT managers should make sure their wishes are heeded. That said, IT should not be run like a

---

[18] Martin Curley, *Managing Information Technology for Business Value: Practical Strategies for IT and Business Managers,* Intel Press (2007).

for-profit business because the quest for IT profitability could undermine the profitability of the larger business. Managing IT like a business creates a closed-loop feedback mechanism for making adjustments and optimizing the system.

One route to IT value is effective IT governance. Citing the research of Peter Weill of MIT, Dr. Curley notes that enterprises with above average IT governance enjoy on average at least 20% higher return on assets than other firms with the same strategic objectives.

In addition to analyzing new business models, enterprises also must develop the capabilities to test the most promising ones. Dr. Curley and Dr. Piero Formica advocate experimental labs or "intellectual supercolliders" where young entrepreneurs come together and share business ideas and grow ideas through business simulation quickly. The goal is to test them in a lab environment before committing capital.

Corporate IT as a Pilot for the Future Internet?

According to Dr. Curley, enterprises should adopt an "IT business value mindset." Business executives should recognize IT as an asset that can transform the business, not merely as a cost center. IT managers must put business value at the forefront of their thinking.

Businesses should continually overinvest in IT. It is the only business resource that delivers twice the capability every eighteen months at a lower or equal cost. But overinvestment should not be confused with profligate spending. Instead, businesses should follow the careful methodologies described above to winnow potential investments and focus on those with the most promise.

IT is changing so rapidly that firms must reinvest on a cyclical schedule. This means planning investments and upgrades and adhering to their plans unless forced to change by unforeseen events. They also should sequence their investments or roll out new technology in phases to maximize its value. Similarly, they should look for compound investments, or those that build upon previous ones and leverage greater value.

The enterprise may serve as a metaphor, or parable, for broader questions related to the Future Internet. When we discuss the Future

Internet, it is not just the corporation or IT department that is at stake; rather, it is global society. Just as the corporate IT department must pursue better business models and governance, the global community must work to create a better model for our societal operating system. If we can demonstrate that governance has a demonstrable benefit in the enterprise, it is reasonable to conclude that good governance might have a positive effect in the open Internet.

New Opportunities

The Future Internet will make it easier to spontaneously form value chains that combine diverse groups of people and technologies. Business webs will enable these groups to assemble and operate. Here are some examples of the types of new services that may become more common in the Future Internet. This list does not represent an exhaustive, all-inclusive tally of all future opportunities; but is simply a sampling of potential opportunities that allows us to imagine how these capabilities may come to fruition.

Human Services

The Future Internet enables new forms of services beyond mere technical, automated services. Dr. Gautam Shroff, Vice President, Tata Consultancy Services and head of TCS Innovation Labs in Delhi, India, predicts that cloud platforms will allow more commoditization of human services delivered over the Internet. Dr. Shroff calls this the "services cloud."

One example is virtual education. An online educational institution could maintain a distributed faculty and do virtually everything online—publish lectures, administer tests, and award degrees. Many examples of this sort of offering already are widely available, such as U21Global, a consortium of 21 universities and faculty that offers graduate programs on the Internet. This takes a business model (higher education) that has changed little in generations and turns it into a cloud service. Dr. Shroff holds up U21Global as just one example of a coming class of services distinguished by pay-per-use, rapid provisioning, and commoditization.

Agent Clouds

Similarly, Dr. Shroff foresees an "agent cloud." Right now, most devices are consumers of services. Laptops, computers, mobile phones, or sensors generally consume services in clouds or networks. In the future, however, these devices will become servers in their own right. This opens the door to new kinds of applications: greener ways to propel vehicles, smart buildings, better surveillance systems, and seamless communication and collaboration with phones, video, and so on.

Precision Retailing

One example of a new business model is an application for retailers that is tested by SAP and Groupe Casino, one of the world's largest food retailers with nearly 11,000 stores in nine countries and nearly 27 billion euros in net sales. The mobile application is designed to serve both customers and retailers.

First, the mobile platform allows customers to use their phones as personal shopping assistants. This gives retailers three opportunities to make sales: targeted special offers, optimized shopping lists, and up-selling or cross-selling based on the customer's selections. The system leverages CRM information about the shopper's personal preferences along with the store's stock inventories to make personalized offers.

This service delivers real-time information to the shopper, such as product information, local promotions, and special offers. For example, a customer might use his mobile device to search the Web for a product or respond to an advertisement. The customer's phone would show detailed product information and customer reviews. At that point, the store could deliver a targeted offer and even guide the customer to a local store that carries that item.

In another example, this platform could help increase conversion rates. Say the customer interacts with the product in the store. Once again, the system would target the customer with a special offer—perhaps taking into account contextual data such as pricing, local availability, and store priorities—and hopefully convince the customer to go ahead and choose that product.

On the back end, the application gives retailers a powerful platform for marketing and analysis. They can direct advertisements and special offers directly to customers most likely to want them. They can analyze their efforts and refine them for better effectiveness. In short, they can practice high-resolution management, or "precision retailing."

But the drivers of these services won't necessarily be cutting-edge technologies; rather these services will be driven by the convergence of mobile networks and the Internet. In other words, this Future Internet won't be entirely futuristic. Rather, the agent cloud will go beyond IP and encompass more mundane networks like phones and SMS. This reflects the reality on the ground: people simply make use of the technologies they have on hand, especially in developing countries. India has almost 400 million mobile phone subscribers but only 40 million Internet users. In one example cited by Dr. Shroff, farmers in rural India use SMS for remote control and monitoring of their irrigation systems at a cost of only 40 euros. This system shows how basic technologies can be linked and turned into effective cloud services.

Business Intelligence

One example of the power of the Future Internet comes out of a joint research project from SAP and Unilever. The consumer products company sought to arm its field staff with more powerful business intelligence for retail execution powered by an "on-demand middleware" that gathers data from backend systems and orchestrates the processes from beginning to end.

Imagine the rep is making calls on potential clients. Before each visit, the rep can hit a few buttons and see the latest business intelligence on that company, including sales, purchasing history, comparison with competitors, product catalogues, and store planograms. When they walk into the client's building, their iPad becomes a display piece that can stream high-resolution demos, product presentations, and commercials.

In another example, the sales representatives might want to know if their product is being properly displayed in local stores. They can use the iPad application to pull up a succinct profile of a store, its products, and local advertising campaigns. The rep might compare the contracted display areas with the actual store displays.

When salespeople head into the field, they carry along a powerful mix of tools—all contained in the device that weighs slightly more than half a kilogram.

Flash Companies

The Future Internet can speed up both the execution of existing business processes, and the entire process of business formation. One intriguing concept is the "flash company,"[19] an ad hoc startup that forms spontaneously around specific initiatives. Increasingly, companies can form in an instant: one person conceives of an idea, another person—or even a crowd—designs it, a third person manufactures it, and so on.

The Future Internet will open up new collaborative networks. At the 2010 International Research Forum, Paul Hawking, SAP Academic Programs Director and Senior Lecturer at the School of Management and Information Systems at Victoria University, held up the idea of business network transformation: entrepreneurship will move from low-value activities to high-value activities and companies will focus on core strengths and outsource the rest. In the process, these companies will develop networks of key partners who specialize in whatever they need.

This means a future where outsourcing is even more common than it is today. Companies need to think in terms of processes and coordination rather than mechanical components.

"The business you want to be in right now is controlling outsourcing," says Dr. Charles Petrie, Senior Research Scientist, Stanford Logic Group, Computer Science Department at Stanford University. "Outsourcing is the efficient business model of the future. Internet capabilities have to be able to support that."

Another potential business model may come from platforms to ignite these flash companies. We are seeing the emergence of services that allow businesses to recruit partners and collaborate.

Dr. Petrie notes that Web 2.0 technologies and web services allow software, as well as people, to be both providers and consumers of services. New technologies are emerging to describe the services and products, combine the services dynamically, and monitor and manage the global consequences of such dynamic interconnectedness.

This process could be facilitated by something that Dr. Petrie calls "Coordination Engineering." People and software applications must be notified about the effects of their actions or changing circumstances. This coordination would resolve conflicts and trigger alerts for threats, synergies, and opportunities.

---

[19] This term, "flash company," was originated by Dr. Charles Petrie in "Plenty of Room Outside the Firm," *IEEE Internet Computing,* January/February, 2010, *http://www-cdr.stanford.edu/~petrie/online/peer2peer/vision2010.pdf.*

"The effects of such a coordinated Internet would be world changing, because we will be able to better manage complexity due to change," says Dr. Petrie. "This will revolutionize how companies are organized, with fewer middle managers and stronger interactions with other companies." In fact, he suggests this may even make fixed companies unnecessary and allow them to be replaced by ad hoc enterprises, such as global relief efforts for catastrophes.

Dr. Petrie foresees many potential examples—not only flash companies but also space projects, dynamic supply chains, or musical bands on tour. As he says, "The ability to better manage complexity will result in projects that are more massive than any contemplated today."

Collective Optimization

The Future Internet might enable services that connect partners in a system that allows for collective optimization while protecting proprietary or private information.

We already have seen the development of business intelligence and optimization schemes capable of operating at large scale. But applying such applications across many participants is another matter. They depend on the ability of the partners (companies or individual citizens) to share information with assurances that it will remain private and secure—even from other contributors.

These services will use information from all partners to optimize a system-wide solution for the benefit of all. Some examples might include optimized traffic flows that make use of itineraries from car navigation systems, utility pricing systems based on individual energy use, or healthcare analyses that draw upon individual medical records.

Prof. Dr. Gerhard Satzger, Director Karlsruhe Service Research Institute, Karlsruhe Institute of Technology (KIT), points out that these applications have several key requirements: individuals will participate only when their information is used for the limited purpose at hand, its distribution is fully controlled, and they have the right to withdraw at any time.

Smart Metering

Smart metering shows how the Future Internet will enable the intelligent integration of people, things, and data. Paul Hawking points out that smart metering leverages several key elements of the Future Internet: the Internet of Things, the Internet of Services, and the Internet of Data.

For example, one Australian electrical utility is rolling out smart metering to approximately a million customers. This system will capture usage data and apply business intelligence technology to improve understanding of usage patterns and planning.

Many additional layers of analysis and data could be layered on top of this platform. For example, meteorological information from government weather agencies could be used to model electricity usage in various weather conditions. Similarly, other government agencies could supply data about solar panel installations to help understand their impact. Mashups could be written to collect and integrate data in real time for predictive modeling and optimization of electrical generation and distribution.

Traffic Monitoring

Traffic monitoring is a prime example of how data may be exploited and remixed into novel applications. Canadian company IMS designs software that uses location data from cell phones to deliver real-time traffic information.

The IMS Metro Traffic Engine captures location data from millions of mobile phones and GPS devices—which report their whereabouts up to twice each second—and repurposes them as anonymous traffic probes. The IMS algorithms determine the paths and speeds of each device. It aggregates this data, calculates average speeds, and estimates travel times between locations. According to the company, the Metro Traffic Engine is as accurate, or more accurate, than loop detectors, radar sensors, and other traffic measurement equipment.

Internet of Things

The Internet of Things is characterized by vast numbers of devices with very "bursty" data volumes and rates. The cloud provides the capacity and elasticity to cope with this variability. The cloud and the Future Internet can provide a venue for applications that require rapid processing and analysis, such as environmental monitoring or healthcare applications.

Conclusion

Business model innovation is a matter of creating novel combinations of processes, technology, and people. For any business small to large, the key is to make this kind of innovation more efficient and fluid. Ideally, enterprises should have the ability to mashup new business models as easily as they now mashup applications. They need a platform that automates the assembly of business models. This is the essence behind the idea of business webs.

These business webs represent assemblies of the puzzle pieces of the Future Internet into coherent solutions. They unite infrastructure, platforms, services, and applications into end-to-end business solutions. These webs must be agile enough to evolve with the changing times. As a result, business models can be aggregated and combined for greater efficiency. They can add new functions to capitalize on new technology or meet new demands. These business webs put business model innovation—and the capabilities of the Future Internet—within reach of any enterprise.

Peering into the Future

The Future Internet will not arrive all at once in a sudden tsunami of change. Rather, it will creep up on us in a flowing, continuous transformation. Substantial challenges lie ahead, including questions of technology, economics, governance, and society. Some will be solved in the near term; others may take many years.

In the first incarnation of the Internet, the architectural design phase involved a relatively small coterie of technologists in a shared environment of trust. The Future Internet must be designed on a vastly larger scale and involve the entire global community. Researchers from government, business, and academia are making advances, but many challenges remain unresolved.

Our responsibility for designing and implementing the Future Internet is unprecedented. The Internet has become a critical infrastructure, one as vital to our lives as traditional infrastructures such as electricity, roads, and telephones. It even has absorbed the functions of some of the previous critical infrastructure.

The Internet is becoming our societal operating system and must meet the requirements embodied in these many roles. The Internet is no longer just a communication network or an ecommerce platform. Now it is the forum for our most vital activities including government, socializing, work, and health. It must meet the needs of the many facets of our identities: citizens, employees, consumers, social animals, and private individuals.

If we can overcome the technical, economic, and political challenges of the Future Internet, we have the opportunity to create one of the most powerful tools in the history of humankind. It will provide a means to address what the European Commission has called the "grand challenges" of our times, including energy production, environment, climate change, water and food, aging societies, public health, pandemics, and security. Similarly, it will serve as a vital tool for business.

The Future Internet represents a horizon when the Internet will become even more important; it will become an omnipresent fact of life that permeates virtually every human activity. We will live in smart homes, connect with friends and family via social networks, conduct business via business webs, and so on.

Today, technology allows almost any activity to be decomposed and conducted remotely. Thanks to advances in networking, virtually any sort of information processing or knowledge work can be performed anywhere, as dictated by the price of labor or location of specialized expertise. The Web is now an infinite mesh that extends across the globe and allows us to form networks with people across political boundaries, oceans, and time zones. We can conduct business across obstacles that seemed insurmountable before this century.

The dawning of the Future Internet also represents a mandate for business. Enterprises must adapt to a future in which the Internet serves as the main marketplace and the platform for managing and doing business. Indeed, it will perform the business functions previously associated with place names: the market, the retail counter, the service station, the office, and the water cooler. Those physical entities that remain—the factory, the warehouse, the shipping container—will increasingly have information shadows in the digital world that report their status in real time.

In order to compete in this new world, enterprises need a platform that brings together all these diverse elements. Business webs are a manifestation of the Future Internet. These business webs represent a new paradigm in which the Internet serves as an omnipresent, ubiquitous part of the business world. These networks will allow enterprises to take advantage of these new capabilities and create products, services, and business models that we cannot currently envision. Today, many of us cannot imagine life without Google, Facebook, or an iPod. A little more than a decade ago, however, we could not imagine life *with* these services. This demonstrates how the powerful combination of technology, creative thinking, and business efficiency can lead us beyond the current horizon.

Business webs allow enterprises to combine and manage the many elements of the Future Internet. As we saw in the previous chapter, the real business value of technology often comes not from the technology itself; rather it comes from the business process improvements and new business models enabled by the technologies. By understanding the opportunities and limits of the underlying technologies, businesses will be better positioned to create their own business models.

The Future Internet represents an intricate puzzle of technical, economic, and social questions. As we have seen, the solutions are not always clear. No business should pick up this volume—or any book, for that matter—with the illusion that they have found a "playbook" for the future. We have tried to describe puzzle pieces that we can already see and gaps that remain unclear. But the future is impossible to predict and those who are too confident in making predictions often prove to be wrong. That said, any business should start thinking about the future and what it means for their enterprise. We may not have all the answers yet, but if we start thinking about the questions now we are more likely to arrive at intelligent answers when the future comes knocking on our door.

Appendix: Participants

Authors

Hervé Couturier is the head of Business Information Technology & Research at SAP AG. He is responsible for driving the company's global research agenda to accelerate the cycle of innovation to business impact. In addition, he delivers technologies to enable customers to flexibly access and extend mission-critical business solutions, incorporating business intelligence solutions that help transform corporate data into meaningful insight. Couturier reports to Vishal Sikka, Chief Technology Officer and Member of the Executive Board, SAP AG.

Couturier joined SAP as a result of the acquisition of Business Objects. Prior to joining Business Objects as head of Development in 2002, he held management positions at a number of IT companies, including S1

Corporation, a provider of software for financial and payment services, from 1998 to 2002, and XRT, a leading European treasury management software company (now part of the Sage Group PLC) from 1997 to 1998. Couturier began his career at IBM in 1982, where he held various engineering and business positions through 1997.

Couturier holds both an engineering degree and a master's degree from the École Centrale Paris in France. He serves on the boards of the software companies SimCorp A/S and AVEVA Group PLC.

Burkhard Neidecker-Lutz is part of the strategy group at SAP Research and technical architect for strategic cross-practice projects. In his previous role as CTO of SAP Research, he worked on in-memory databases and helped to shape SAP's cloud computing strategy.

Before joining SAP he held positions with the research departments of Digital Equipment and Compaq. In his 20-year professional career he has worked on diverse topics ranging from multimedia systems, document standards, database engine design, to cloud computing. He's a member of the ACM Europe Council, the industrial chair of the European Cloud Expert Group, and holds a master's degree in computer science from the University of Karlsruhe.

Dr. Vasco Alexander Schmidt is a mathematician, linguist, and science writer working for SAP Research Communications. Vasco writes about research projects focusing on Future Energy, the Internet of Services, and the Future Internet. His interests include technical communication, linguistics, and the sociology of science and technology. He has been a visiting lecturer at various universities, including the University of Heidelberg and the University of Siegen (Germany). Vasco contributes domain expertise in mathematics to the Language and Knowledge research network, an interdisciplinary research initiative on language and knowledge based at the University of Heidelberg.

Dan Woods is a seasoned CTO, author, speaker, and entrepreneur with broad experience in business, computer science, journalism, and publishing. Dan holds an M.S. from Columbia University's Graduate School of Journalism and a B.A. in Computer Science from the University of Michigan. Dan has written 20 books about technology-related topics and writes a weekly column for *Forbes.com*. In 2002, Dan founded Evolved Media, a technology communications and analysis firm serving companies from startups to the Fortune 100. In 2009, Dan founded CITO Research, a community-based research organization serving the needs of CIOs, CTOs, and other IT professionals.

Participants

Dr. Martin Curley is Director of Intel Labs Europe and a senior principal engineer at Intel Corporation. Most recently Martin was Global Director of IT Innovation at Intel Corporation. Previously he held a number of senior IT Management positions for Intel and held management and research positions at General Electric and Philips. Martin has a degree in Electronic Engineering, a Masters in Business Studies from University College Dublin, Ireland, and a PhD in Information Systems from the National University of Ireland, Maynooth.

Martin is author or co-author of three books on technology management for value, innovation, and entrepreneurship. He is also Professor of Technology and Business Innovation at the National University of Ireland, Maynooth and co-founder/Director of the Innovation Value Institute, helping to lead a unique industry-academic open-innovation consortium to advance IT management and innovation. Martin is a fellow of the Institution of Engineers of Ireland, the British Computer Society, and the Irish Computer Society, and has been a visiting scholar at MIT Sloan.

Prof. Dr. Oliver Günther is Dean of the School of Business and Economics at Humboldt University, Berlin, Germany. He also directs Humboldt's Institute of Information Systems and its Interdisciplinary Center on Ubiquitous Information. Prof. Günther has held visiting appointments at the European School of Management and Technology, Tsinghua University in Beijing, ENST Paris, UC Berkeley, the University of Cape Town, and, most recently, at SAP Labs in Palo Alto. He served as an IT strategy consultant and board member to numerous government agencies and high-tech companies. His current research interests include business applications of social networks, RFID architectures, IT productivity, and security and privacy in ubiquitous computing.

Paul Hawking is a Senior Lecturer in Information Systems at Victoria University in Australia. He is one of the leading commentators on ERP systems, specifically SAP solutions. His knowledge is well respected in both industry and academia and accordingly he is often required to assist companies with their ERP strategies and understanding of SAP solutions. He has presented at Sapphire, ASUG, and SAUG conferences. He is an "Expert Blogger" on the SAP Community Network. He trains and advises academics around the world in regard to ERP systems curriculum. He was a past Chairperson and committee member of the SAP Australian User Group (SAUG) and was responsible for knowledge transfer. He now designs and advises the SAUG on the content for their events. In 2009 and 2011, Paul was voted by the SAP community as one of the Top Ten Most Influential People in SAP for Australia and New Zealand. In 2010 he became a SAP Mentor and is the only academic to achieve this status.

Paul is also one Australia's bestselling IT authors, having written ten books that are sold throughout the world. His areas of teaching and research include ERP systems, strategy and implementation, and business intelligence. He has published more than 100 research papers in leading conferences and journals.

Prof. Dr. Lutz Heuser is the CEO of AGT Germany and CTO of AGT International, where he leads R&D activity for all of AGT. He has a PhD from the Technical University of Karlsruhe and is an adjunct Professor at the Queensland University of Technology, Brisbane. He is Vice-Chairman of ISTAG (Advisory Group for ICT to the European Commission). Heuser is one of the world's leading innovators in Information and Communication Technologies (ICT), and is regarded as a Research and Development entrepreneur. Prior to AGT, he worked as Global Head of SAP Research, where he built up one of the leading European industrial research organizations in ICT.

Prof. Dr. Max Mühlhäuser is head of the Telecooperation Lab at Technische Universität Darmstadt, Informatics Dept. The Lab works on smart ubiquitous computing environments for the "pervasive Internet" in three research fields: middleware/infrastructures, novel multimodal interaction techniques, and IT security/civil security. He also heads the "RBG" division for e-Learning and computing services. As directorate member of CASED, the Center for Advanced Security Research Darmstadt, he heads the Secure Services division and a special group on civil security. Max is responsible for a university-wide PhD program in E-Learning and is instrumental in collaborative research on Adaptive and Peer-to-Peer networks funded by the national funding agency DFG. His academic and technology transfer appointments include chair of the academic steering committee at SAP Research, CEC Darmstadt lab.

Max has about 25 years of experience in research and teaching in areas related to Ubiquitous Computing (UC), Networks and Distributed Systems, and E-Learning. He held professorships at the Universities of Kaiserslautern, Karlsruhe, Linz, Darmstadt, Montréal, Sophia Antipolis, and San Diego (UCSD). In 1993, he founded the TeCO institute *(www.teco .edu)* in Karlsruhe, Germany. Max regularly publishes in *Ubiquitous and Distributed Computing, HCI, Multimedia,* and E-Learning conferences and journals and has authored or co-authored over 300 publications. He is a reviewer for some 15 conferences per year, organizer of several annual conferences, member of editorial boards or guest editor in journals like *Pervasive Computing, ACM Multimedia, Pervasive and Mobile Computing, Web Engineering,* and *Distance Learning Technology.*

Dr. Charles Petrie is a Senior Research Scientist working in the Stanford CS Logic Group. His research topics are concurrent engineering, enterprise management, and collective work. Dr. Petrie was a Founding Member of Technical Staff of the MCC AI Lab, Founding Editor-in-Chief of IEEE Internet Computing, and Founding Executive Director of the Stanford Networking Research Center. He is the Founding Chair of the Semantic Web Services Challenge. He received his PhD in Computer Science from The University of Texas at Austin.

Dr. Petrie collaborates with STI Innsbruck and DERI Galway and was recently an Advisor to SAP's Enterprise Services Community. He has also consulted with companies such as HP, Siemens, Volkswagen, DaimlerChrysler, CommerceNet, and Commerce One on advanced IT technologies. He has been a member of the Technology Advisory Group of DaimlerChrysler. He has worked on Stanford projects with SAP and some of the POEM project results are now reflected in SAP products.

Prof. Dr. Gerhard Satzger is Director of the Karlsruhe Service Research Institute, an innovative "industry-on-campus" institution founded by IBM and the Karlsruhe Institute of Technology (KIT) in Germany. He heads the research group "Service Innovation & Management." His research interests are the development and management of IT-based and IT-supported services. Prof. Satzger is actively involved in the development of service research, serving also on task forces for the federally funded High-Tech-Strategy in Germany as well as a number of academic and industry boards.

Prior to his appointment in Karlsruhe, Prof. Satzger was CFO of IBM's Global Technology Services business in Germany and other parts of Europe and has a broad background of national and international management positions in IBM. He obtained a PhD ("Habilitation") from the University of Augsburg based on his work on "Capital intensive services in global markets," after receiving a PhD in Information Systems from the University of Giessen and an MBA from Oregon State University, US. Prof. Satzger graduated from the University of Karlsruhe with a degree in Business Engineering.

Dr. Joachim Schaper is Vice President Research, AGT. After graduating in Computer Science at the TU Karlsruhe, Joachim had a full-time position at Daimler-Benz in system design. He joined the campus-based research center (later known as the European Applied Research Center, EARC) of Digital Equipment GmbH as a member of the research team, responsible for user interfaces, object-oriented modeling, and design of teaching and learning systems. He completed his PhD in computer science at the TU Karlsruhe working for DEC in the area of computer-assisted learning, taking the director position of CEC Karlsruhe in 1997. Since 1999, Joachim has been Director of SAP's research group, CEC Karlsruhe as part of SAP AG's corporate research. He is responsible for research programs including: E-Learning, Smart-Items, Mobile Computing, Technology for Application Integration, and Advanced Customer Interfaces. Joachim was Vice President of Americas from 2003–2005, developing the SAP Research group in Palo Alto. Since 2005 he was Vice President of EMEA for SAP Research, developing new groups in Pretoria, Darmstadt, Dresden, and Belfast, guiding the strategic technology research in the EMEA region. Since December 2010 Joachim is heading the research organization of AGT.

Dr. Gautam Shroff heads TCS' Innovation Lab in Delhi, which conducts applied research in software architecture, natural language processing, multimedia, and graphics. Additionally he is responsible for TCS' Co-Innovation Network, which works with emerging technology companies to create and take to market solutions that have disruptive innovation potential. As a member of TCS' Corporate Technology Board, he is also involved in the process of recommending directions to existing R&D efforts, spawning new R&D efforts, sponsoring external research, and proliferating the resulting technology and intellectual property across TCS' businesses.

Prior to joining TCS in 1998, Dr. Shroff had been on the faculty of the California Institute of Technology, Pasadena, US, after which he joined the Department of Computer Science and Engineering at Indian Institute of Technology, Delhi, India.

Dr. Shroff has a B.Tech degree in Electrical Engineering from the Indian Institute of Technology, Kanpur, India (1985), and a PhD in Computer Science from Rensselaer Polytechnic Institute, NY, US (1990).

Dr. David Skellern (FTSE FIEEE HonFIEAust) has worked on electronic and information systems design and development, including hardware and software, throughout his career. He retired in 2011 after six years as CEO of National ICT Australia Ltd, Australia's 700-person national research center for information and communications technologies.

Dr. Skellern spent ten years from 1974 designing, building, and commissioning extensions to the Fleurs Synthesis Radiotelescope before joining the academic staff at Sydney University's Electrical Engineering Department. In 1989 he moved to Macquarie University as Professor and Head of Electronics. While an academic, he worked in industry as a visiting researcher, including some three years at Hewlett-Packard Laboratories.

In 1997 he co-founded Radiata Inc, which demonstrated the world's first IEEE 802.11a chip-set in September 2000. Radiata was acquired by Cisco Systems, where he was Technology Director of Cisco's Wireless Networking Business Unit until 2004.

Dr Skellern holds BSc, BE, and PhD degrees and is an author or co-author of 5 patents and over 180 journal and conference papers.

Professor Dr. Wolfgang Wahlster is the Director and CEO of the German Research Center for Artificial Intelligence (DFKI) and a Professor of Computer Science at Saarland University. He has published more than 180 technical papers and 9 books on user modeling, language technology, intelligent user interfaces, the semantic web and instrumented environments. He is an AAAI Fellow (elected in 1993), an ECCAI Fellow (since 1999), and a GI Fellow (since 2004). In 2001, the President of Germany presented the German Future Prize to Professor Wahlster for his work on language technology and intelligent user interfaces. He was the first German computer scientist elected Foreign Member of the Royal Swedish Academy of Sciences, Stockholm 2003. In 2004, he was elected Full Member of the German National Academy of Sciences Leopoldina, founded in 1652. In 2006, he was awarded the Federal Cross of Merit, First Class of Germany. He has also been appointed a member of the Research Union "Business-Science" as chief advisor for ICT research by the German government. Since 2009 he has been a member of the Executive Steering Board of the EIT ICT Labs of the European Institute of Innovation and Technology.

Virtual Participants

Thomas Michael Bohnert is Technical Director at SAP Research. His interests are focused on enabling ICT infrastructures for enterprises. At SAP this covers cloud computing, service oriented infrastructure, and carrier-grade service delivery platforms (Telco + IT).

Over the past years he has shaped SAP's Future Internet vision as founder of the "Future Internet Research Alliance" and owner of SAP's engagement in the European Future Internet Public-Private-Partnership. In this capacity he shaped SAP Research's prime event, the International Research Forum 2010, which runs under the heading "Future Internet" and is a prime source for this book.

Before joining SAP he worked for John Deere & Company, Siemens Corporate Technology, and ran an IT consultancy named BNCS. He was a visiting scholar with Tampere University of Technology, NEC Network Research Labs, VTT Technical Research Centre, and Beijing University of Posts and Telecommunications.

His works have been published in several books, journals, and conferences. He regularly serves as reviewer for the *IEEE Communications Magazine* and serves as regional correspondent (Europe) for the magazine's news section.

He is the founder of the IEEE Broadband Wireless Access Workshop and is a steering board member of the European technology platform eMobility.

As member of the FI-PPP's architecture board he continues to shape Europe's Future Internet vision on behalf of SAP.

Dr. David Clark is a Senior Research Scientist at the MIT Computer Science and Artificial Intelligence Laboratory, where he has worked since receiving his PhD there in 1973. Since the mid 70s, Dr. Clark has been leading the development of the Internet. From 1981–1989 he acted as Chief Protocol Architect in this development, and chaired the Internet Activities Board. His current research looks at the re-definition of the architectural underpinnings of the Internet, and the relation of technology and architecture to economic, societal, and policy considerations. He is helping the US National Science foundation organize their Future Internet Design program. Dr. Clark is past chairman of the Computer Science and Telecommunications Board of the National Academies, and has contributed to a number of studies on the societal and policy impact of computer communications. He is co-director of the MIT Communications Futures Program, a project for industry collaboration and coordination along the communications value chain.

Dr. Paul Hofmann is Vice President, Group of the Chief Scientist, SAP Labs at Palo Alto. Before joining the Chief Scientist, Paul worked for the SAP Corporate Venturing Group.

Paul joined SAP in 2001 as Director Strategic Supply Chain Management Initiative EMEA. His pre-sales team designed and rolled out the SCM Value Based Selling Approach for EMEA and supported many crucial Supply Chain sales.

Prior to joining SAP, he was Senior Plant Manager at BASF's Global Catalysts Business Unit. Paul headed the development of object-oriented production planning and scheduling software for BASF's plants; one of the first big object-oriented software projects in German industry. He also developed an AI System for Catalysts.

Paul was a researcher and Assistant Professor at top universities, such as Northwestern University in Evanston/Chicago, Illinois, US and Technical University in Munich, Germany.

At Northwestern he did computer simulations to explain molecular beam reactions. He used Cray supercomputers extensively for this work and collaborated with Sir John Pople (Nobel Prize Laureate).

Paul studied Chemistry and Physics at the University of Vienna, Austria. He received a Bachelor in biotechnology and a master's degree in chemistry. He did his PhD in Physics at the Darmstadt University of Technology, Germany.

He is the author of numerous publications and books.

Dr. Hagen Hultzsch, formerly Executive Board Member and CTO of Deutsche Telekom, has more than 45 years of experience in information and telecommunications technology. He served as Assistant Professor at Mainz University. After a leave of absence to IBM's Thomas J. Watson Research Centre, he headed the Computing Centre of GSI in Darmstadt and thereafter became Director of the Technical Services Group at Electronic Data Systems in Germany. Later, he joined Volkswagen AG in Wolfsburg as Corporate Executive Director for Organization and Information Systems.

Dr. Hultzsch serves on the boards or advisory boards of a series of companies, including T-Systems Solutions for Research, Radware, Zimory, TeleSoftVC, University Medical Hospitals Bonn and Dresden, Fraunhofer Fokus. He also serves or served on national and international bodies, including DFN, DFG, EARN, Share Europe, BDI, FZJ, Münchner Kreis, Bundesvereinigung Logistik, FGF, EFQM, ICANN, TranSwitch, SCM-Microsystems, RIT Technologies, living-e, AuthentiDate, SAP CEC Research Council, Gemini Israel Fund, and Dresden and Frankfurt University Boards of Trusties.

Dr. Roger Kilian-Kehr is Head of the SAP Research Practice "Software Engineering and Tools." After receiving his diploma in Computer Science from Darmstadt University of Technology in 1997, Roger joined Net & Publication Consultance GmbH, a small consulting company working on software development projects and security solutions for the financial sector. From 1999 until 2002 he was research assistant at the Databases and Distributed Systems Group at Darmstadt University and research project manager at the Research and Development Center of Deutsche Telekom AG, Darmstadt, Germany, with a focus on ICT Security. While there, he participated in a number of joint projects with other European telecommunication providers. He obtained his Doctoral degree in Computer Science from Darmstadt University in 2002 in architectures and technologies for mobile security with smart cards. Roger joined SAP Research in 2002 as a Research Project Manager. From 2004 until 2010, he was Research Program Manager of the Research Program "Software and Service Engineering and Architecture."

Volkmar Lotz has more than 20 years experience in industrial research on security and software engineering. He is leading the Security & Trust Research practice of SAP Research, a group of 40 researchers working on innovative security solutions for business applications, services, and platforms. His responsibilities include the definition and execution of SAP's security research agenda, its strategic alignment to SAP's business needs, and the maintenance of a global research partner network. His current research interests include business process security, service security, authorization, security engineering, and compliance. Volkmar has published numerous scientific papers in his area of interest and is regularly serving on program committees of internationally renowned conferences. Volkmar holds a diploma in Computer Science from the University of Kaiserslautern.

Prof. Martin Przewloka serves as Senior Vice President at SAP and is responsible for the Global SAP Research Program of Future Internet Applications and Services.

During his tenure with SAP, Prof. Przewloka held various management roles. Previously, he was the Senior Vice President of Showcase & Trial Solutions as part of SAP Marketing; responsible world-wide for all SAP demo and presentation solutions, infrastructures, and services. Formerly, Prof. Przewloka was responsible for several SAP industry solutions as well as for SAP ERP, the SAP flagship product.

Prof. Przewloka is based at the SAP headquarters in Walldorf Germany. Additionally, he holds university degrees in physics, economics, and medical science from the universities of Giessen/Germany, Geneva/Switzerland, and Kaiserslautern/Germany. Furthermore, he holds a professorship in mathematics from the Technische Hochschule Mittelhessen/Germany and a professorship in computer sciences from the Provadis School of International Management & Technology Frankfurt/Germany.

 **Dr. Karsten Schulz** is the Program Director, Vice President, and Founder of SAP Research Centre, Brisbane and Sydney, Australia, and Adjunct Associate Professor at the University of Queensland, Australia. He holds a PhD in Computer Science from the University of Queensland, and a BA in Electrical Engineering from the University of Furtwangen in Germany.

In his current role, Karsten oversees SAP's research in business network orchestration and is actively involved in SAP's global internal and external research with a strong focus on the Asia-Pacific Region. He is member of SAP Research's Executive Leadership Team and executive sponsor of several research topics at SAP Research. Karsten's research interests include business process management, mobile computing, user experience, user collaboration, robotics, and quantum computing.

www.ingramcontent.com/pod-product-compliance
Lightning Source LLC
Chambersburg PA
CBHW051254050326
40689CB00007B/1190